This Book is
Protected by
Instant IP

GIFTED

ON PURPOSE | FOR PURPOSE

GIFTED

ON PURPOSE | FOR PURPOSE

Matt Dawson

ethos
collective

GIFTED © 2026 by Matthew T. Dawson. All rights reserved.

Printed in the United States of America

Published by Igniting Souls
PO Box 43, Powell, OH 43065
IgnitingSouls.com

This book contains material protected under international and federal copyright laws and treaties. Any unauthorized reprint or use of this material is prohibited. No part of this book may be reproduced or transmitted in any form or by any means, electronic or mechanical, including photocopying, recording, or by any information storage and retrieval system, without express written permission from the author.

LCCN: 2025926840
Paperback ISBN: 978-1-63680-581-8
Hardcover ISBN: 978-1-63680-582-5
e-Book ISBN: 978-1-63680-583-2
Available in paperback, hardcover, e-book, and audiobook.

Unless otherwise indicated, all Scripture quotations are taken from the Holy Bible, New Living Translation, copyright ©1996, 2004, 2007, 2013, 2015 by Tyndale House Foundation. Used by permission of Tyndale House Publishers, Inc., Carol Stream, Illinois 60188. All rights reserved.

Scripture quotations marked MSG are taken from The Message, copyright © 1993, 2002, 2018 by Eugene H. Peterson. Used by permission of NavPress. All rights reserved. Represented by Tyndale House Publishers.

Scripture quotations marked NKJV are taken from the New King James Version®. Copyright © 1982 by Thomas Nelson. Used by permission. All rights reserved.

Scripture quotations marked NASB are taken from the (NASB®) New American Standard Bible®, Copyright © 1960, 1971, 1977, 1995, 2020 by The Lockman Foundation. Used by permission. All rights reserved. lockman.org

Any Internet addresses (websites, blogs, etc.) and telephone numbers printed in this book are offered as a resource. They are not intended in any way to be or imply an endorsement by Igniting Souls, nor does Igniting Souls vouch for the content of these sites and numbers for the life of this book.

Some names and identifying details may have been changed to protect the privacy of individuals.

The content of this book reflects the author's personal experiences, opinions, and interpretations. The inclusion of any individual, living or deceased, or any organization or entity, is not intended to malign, defame, or harm the reputation of such persons or entities. All statements regarding individuals are solely the author's perspective and do not represent verified facts unless expressly cited to a verifiable source.

The publisher has not independently investigated or confirmed the accuracy of any such references and disclaims all responsibility for them. Nothing in this book should be construed as factual assertions about the character, conduct, or reputation of any individual or entity mentioned. Any resemblance to persons living or dead is purely coincidental unless explicitly stated.

The publisher expressly disclaims liability for any alleged loss, damage, or injury arising from any perceived defamatory content or reliance upon statements within this work. Responsibility for the views, depictions, and representations rests solely with the author.

The superscript symbol IP listed throughout this book is known as the unique certification mark created and owned by Instant IP®. Its use signifies that the corresponding expression (words, phrases, chart, graph, etc.) has been protected by Instant IP® via smart contract. Instant IP® is designed with the patented smart contract solution (US Patent: 11,928,748), which creates an immutable time-stamped first layer and fast layer identifying the moment in time an idea is filed on the blockchain. This solution can be used in defending intellectual property protection. Infringing upon the respective intellectual property, i.e., IP, is subject to and punishable in a court of law.

To the GIFTED partners at Journey Church and to every GIFTED believer that I've had the privilege of learning and growing from. Thank You!

*God has given each of you a **gift** from his great variety of spiritual gifts. Use them well to serve one another.*

1 Peter 4:10

TABLE OF CONTENTS

Preface xi

PART 1: THE DIVINE DESIGN

1 | The Devil's in the Misunderstandings. 3
2 | ON Purpose FOR Purpose. 11
3 | What Gifts? 19
4 | The Meaning and Purpose of Life. 32
5 | Gifted for Transformation. 46
6 | Gifted for Impact 58

PART 2: YOUR GIFTS PROFILE

7 | Motivational Gifts 71
8 | Ministry Gifts. 106
9 | Manifestation Gifts. 133

PART 3: LIVING GIFTED

10 | Myths and Misconceptions:
 Clearing the Path to Your Purpose 183

11 | Striving in Your Lane:
     Where Your Gifts Meet the World's Needs 205
12 | The Gifted Mirror Test^{IP} 229
13 | What's Next? 237

Endnotes 243
Acknowledgments 245
About the Author 249

PREFACE

Have you ever noticed how Jesus never wasted a moment? Think about that hot, dusty day when he sat at Jacob's well in Samaria. His disciples had gone for takeout (first-century style), and there he was—bone-tired from the journey—when she showed up.

You know her story. The Samaritan woman. The noon-hour water-gatherer. The one avoiding the whispers and side glances of the morning crowd. Five husbands deep and living with number six without the ceremony.

Jesus had no business talking to her. Jewish men didn't chat with Samaritan women, especially ones with her reputation. But Jesus saw more than her past; he saw her purpose.

Their conversation? It's the stuff of divine choreography. He asks for water, then offers her living water. She's talking about buckets and wells, and he's talking about eternities and souls.

When his disciples return, sandwiches in hand, they find Jesus different. Refreshed. Energized. They urge him, "Rabbi, eat something!"

His response? It's the heart of what this entire book is about:

> "I have food to eat that you know nothing about... My food is to do the will of him who sent me and to finish his work" (John 4:32, 34).

Let that sink in.

Jesus found his deepest nourishment not in bread but in purpose. Not in consumption but in commission. Not in getting but in giving.

While his body craved sustenance, his spirit feasted on something greater—the fulfillment of operating precisely within his divine design. Jesus wasn't just checking religious boxes. He wasn't accumulating spiritual brownie points. He was living exactly as he was created to live—ON purpose FOR purpose—and it fed his soul in ways that physical food never could.

I wonder how many of us are spiritually malnourished while our gifts sit unused.

I wonder how many of us keep returning to the well at noon, carrying the same empty jar, drawing the same temporary satisfaction, when what we really crave is the living water of purpose.

I've watched believers with extraordinary gifts live ordinary lives because they never understood that their gifts weren't collectibles to be admired but tools to be wielded. I've seen people with the gift of encouragement scroll through social media complaining about the world rather than speaking life into the disheartened. I've witnessed those with leadership gifts remain silent when God was positioning them to speak up.

Could it be that your deepest dissatisfaction isn't about what's missing from your life but what's dormant within you?

We Have All Been Gifted

The primary reason I wrote this book is to help every reader become aware of the GIFTS they have been given by their heavenly Father, who loves them. The expression of these Gifts given to us is to help **transform our lives**, make an **impact on**

others' lives, and **fulfill the unique purpose** God has for each of us individually.

However, over the last 20+ years of my ministry within the Western church, I've noticed that many believers view these GIFTS as something given to collect, preserve, or protect. They're not sure how their gifts *function* in their everyday lives, so they become something sacred—something that only applies to spiritual contexts. If we're not careful, we can prize these gifts but treat them as something to protect in glass cases. We are grateful to God for giving us these gifts, but we fail to *use* them and instead simply *preserve* them as something we might use "one day" for Him.

Make no mistake, the GIFTS entrusted to every follower of Christ are to be *used*! They are not only practical, but when living a life on mission for God, they are your functional strengths. They are so functional, powerful, and practical that they could be better described as muscles. They are *given* in their basic form but must be exercised, trained, and pushed to their limits in order to grow. As we mature in our understanding of spiritual gifts, we should equally grow in the expression of those gifts in every area of our lives.

Think about Jesus at that well again. He could have sat there in silence, conserving his energy and avoiding the cultural awkwardness. Instead, he activated his gifts—his discernment to see her heart, his wisdom to navigate the conversation, his prophetic insight to reveal her story—and what happened? A woman left her water jar at the well (the very reason she came!) and an entire village came to faith.

When was the last time your gifts made you forget what you originally came for?

We have all been GIFTED… Gifts to USE, not PRESERVE.

What Gifts?

A relationship with Jesus is Gift #1.

The most precious gift of all was that God sent his one and only Son into the world (John 1) to bring light and life to those in darkness. He lived a sinless life as our example, died a criminal's death that we deserve, and rose again to give us victory over death, hell, and the grave! Romans 8:3 tells us that *"the law of Moses was unable to save us because of the weakness of our sinful nature. So God did what the law could not do. He sent His own Son in the body like the bodies we sinners have, and in that body God declared an end to sin's control over us by giving His Son as a sacrifice for our sins."* Our best response to this precious gift of grace is to *accept it*, to surrender our lives for the life He gave us, accepting Jesus as our Savior, and to live our lives for His fame and for the freedom of others in Christ.

Once we have become followers (New Testament language: "disciple") of Jesus, the Holy Spirit of God indwells us. The power of Jesus Christ through His Spirit now lives in us and through us.

The way the Holy Spirit expresses this power in and through our lives is by entrusting us with GIFTS given to us by God. The entire Trinity is at work when it comes to gifting His children (as we will discover in this book), and *everyone* who has the Holy Spirit alive in them has been GIFTED!

While this language of spiritual gifts is common in most churches, there appears to be a significant difference in how people understand and express their gifts in their lives. Some churches center their entire theological ministry and methodology around the practice and expression of spiritual gifts. Some churches discuss these gifts only in the context of professional ministry and in service to the church. Some churches won't discuss "some" spiritual gifts because their methodology of ministry and theology of God don't match very well. There are also some that simply don't discuss spiritual gifts, and I'm not entirely sure why or how they can effectively teach the New Testament and avoid the topic.

No matter your denominational history, theological bent, or affinity for one method of ministry, *everyone* has been GIFTED by God ON purpose FOR purpose!

You don't have to agree with 100 percent of what this book teaches, nor do you have to change your church, denomination, or affiliation to begin living a life that expresses the gifts that you've been given.

My prayer for you is that you will take *one more step* toward living the GIFTED LIFE you've been entrusted with by God. May this book help you take that step.

I believe with every fiber of my being that your greatest satisfaction won't come from a promotion, a relationship, or a purchase. It will come when—like Jesus at that well—you're so engaged in using your gifts for their intended purpose that you forget about your own needs.

When someone asks, "Aren't you tired? Aren't you hungry?" you'll smile and say, "I have food you know nothing about."

That's the feast that awaits when you live ON purpose FOR purpose.

Are you ready to be nourished like never before?

PART 1

The Divine Design

1

THE DEVIL'S IN THE MISUNDERSTANDINGS

I love the movie *The Man Who Knew Too Little*. It's one of Bill Murray's top five comedies to date, in my opinion. The entire premise of the movie is that an American visiting England gets caught up in what he "thinks" is an interactive citywide theater production called "The Theater of Life." But he becomes embroiled in a real cloak-and-dagger spy conflict between Cold War rivals involving blackmail and an attempted assassination.

There are several moments in the movie when Bill's character asks for a "do-over" in the midst of a real-life situation that he thinks is just interactive theater. Again, it's one of his best comedy performances to date!

Throughout the movie (all the way to the end credits), his character has *no idea* that real-life events have transpired during his one night with "The Theater of Life."

Watching a movie about a character who is clueless can be amusing. However, watching people we know and love walk through life, completely missing what's actually going on around them, is entirely different.

That's one of the heartbeats of this book. That we would wake up to truly see our lives the way God sees them, and to fully understand the power He has given us to live our lives "to the full" (John 10:10), or I say in this book, **ON purpose FOR purpose!**

> *Have you ever wondered what your life would look like if you could see it through God's eyes? Imagine the clarity and confidence you'd have if you could recognize the purpose behind every gift He's placed within you. This isn't just about living a better life—it's about living the exact life He designed you for.*

"I DO NOT WANT YOU TO MISUNDERSTAND THIS"

These are Paul's words in his first letter to the church of Corinth. Paul addressed several issues in his letter concerning the church that was gathering in Corinth and the challenges they were facing as the people (ecclesia) of God.

In the last pages of the letter, he began to address the GIFTEDNESS of God's people in the church at Corinth and what seemed to be some areas of misunderstanding.

> *"Now, dear brothers and sisters, regarding your question about the special abilities the Spirit gives us. I don't want you to misunderstand this"* (1 Corinthians 12:1).

Always remember that when Paul wrote his letters, he usually wrote in response to something he had heard or read about the church or the person he was writing to. In this case, Paul was clear about addressing questions that they had about GIFTS.

He devoted the next several hundred words to helping the church recognize the purpose and power that comes with understanding their GIFTEDNESS through the Holy Spirit.

Paul tells us that all GIFTS come from *one God*. I believe that a trinitarian doctrine (God being *three persons* in *one*) is necessary to understand how and why God, through the Holy Spirit, gives these varieties of gifts, but remains *one source* of them all.

> *"There are different kinds of spiritual gifts, but the same Spirit is the source of them all. There are different kinds of service, but we serve the same Lord. God works in different ways, but it is the same God who does the work in all of us"* (1 Corinthians 12:4–6).

He then listed some of the specific gifts given to us by the Holy Spirit. I will break these down in Chapters 3 and 9, so I'm not going to unpack each one of them here. The gifts listed are: Wisdom, Special Knowledge (for a message to others), Faith, Healing, Miracles, Prophecy, Discernment (distinguishing between spirits), Tongues, and Interpretation of Tongues.

The largest portion of this section is not a detailed explanation of what each gift does and does not do. Remember the point of this part of Paul's letter. It was to help God's church understand the *purpose* of these gifts.

He made it clear in the following verse why we are GIFTED.

> *"A spiritual gift is given to each of us so we can help each other"* (1 Corinthians 12:7).

This verse reveals the heart of God's design—your gifts aren't just for you. They were strategically placed within you ON purpose *FOR* purpose. Every ability, every talent, every spiritual gift you possess was intentionally crafted by God to serve a greater function in His kingdom. When we miss this truth, we miss the entire point of our giftedness.

Several passages in the "What Gifts?" chapter will also help us understand *why* God has gifted us, but let's stick with the flow of this letter and stay in 1 Corinthians.

After listing the nine manifestation gifts, Paul emphasized that "(11) It is the one and only Spirit who distributes all these gifts. He alone decides which gift each person should have." Who gets what? God decides. It's one Spirit, of one God, who determines our GIFTEDNESS. This is *very important* for understanding the visual example he provides in the next several verses.

THE DEVIL'S IN THE MISUNDERSTANDINGS

I'm not sure if this phrase was one that you grew up with, but I heard it often. Sometimes it would be re-stated like this, "our enemy thrives in confusion, but our God is a God of order and clarity." You may not agree with that statement, but it meant a great deal to me on my faith journey. While I cannot say that God is always "clear" on something, He is not the "author of confusion" (1 Corinthians 14:33).

One reason I believe Paul spent so much time addressing the topic of GIFTEDNESS with the church in Corinth is that the Enemy of all believers was wreaking havoc through the confusion and misunderstanding of the gifts given to His people. We read later that people were jealous of others and their giftedness. Some saw certain gifts as "more important" than others. Many even assumed that some gifts were unnecessary.

It's not a stretch to say that the 21st-century Western church has lost its understanding of the GIFTS God has given His people. There are several denominations that highlight and magnify certain gifts (usually the "supernatural" gifts) above others, while others don't speak about or teach them at all. Our Western church culture lives at opposite extremes, overcorrecting in theology and methodology, and avoiding association with one another because of vast differences in doctrine regarding Spiritual Gifts.

We're living in a culture of misunderstanding. I believe that the enemy of our souls STILL creates confusion around our understanding and application of our GIFTS, and would rather have us fight amongst ourselves or remain ignorant of the power within each one of us to live with the purpose God has called us to.

I witnessed this firsthand while leading a small-group study on spiritual gifts. A young woman discovered she had the gift of prophecy, but immediately shrank back, saying, "I can't have that gift—our family doesn't believe in that." The enemy had successfully convinced her entire faith community that certain gifts weren't for today, robbing her of the opportunity to step into her divine purpose. The look of both wonder and confusion on her face revealed the battle happening within—recognizing God's gift while simultaneously feeling forbidden to use it.

Paul clarified the purpose and function of our GIFTEDNESS.

> *The human body has many parts, but the many parts make up one whole body. So it is with the body of Christ. Some of us are Jews, some are Gentiles, some are slaves, and some are free. But we have all been baptized into one body by one Spirit, and we all share the same Spirit.*
>
> *Yes, the body has many different parts, not just one part. If the foot says, "I am not a part of the body because I am not a hand," that does not make it any less a part of the body. And if the ear says, "I am not part of the body because I am not an eye," would that make it any less a part of the body? If the whole body were an eye, how would you hear? Or if your whole body were an ear, how would you smell anything?*

> *But our bodies have many parts, and God has put each part just where he wants it. How strange a body would be if it had only one part! Yes, there are many parts, but only one body. The eye can never say to the hand, "I don't need you." The head can't say to the feet, "I don't need you."*
>
> *In fact, some parts of the body that seem weakest and least important are actually the most necessary. And the parts we regard as less honorable are those we clothe with the greatest care. So we carefully protect those parts that should not be seen, while the more honorable parts do not require this special care. So God has put the body together such that extra honor and care are given to those parts that have less dignity. This makes for harmony among the members, so that all the members care for each other. If one part suffers, all the parts suffer with it, and if one part is honored, all the parts are glad.*
>
> *All of you together are Christ's body, and each of you is a part of it* (1 Corinthians 12:12–27).

I cannot reframe this teaching about purpose and power any better than Paul does. Read this passage as many times as necessary until you lock it into your memory. The content and challenge of this entire book rest on your understanding of these fifteen verses.

"SO IT IS WITH THE BODY OF CHRIST!"

To properly understand our individual GIFTEDNESS, we must place it within the context of the body of Christ! Just like the human body, we have many individual parts, different in form and function, but *necessary* to the whole.

The purpose of our giftedness is to work together (help each other) to display the body of Christ. Every gift has a necessary function to help the "body" remain strong. There are *no* inessential parts of the body of Christ! You have been GIFTED to fit within this body and to make the body strong.

I love the way Eugene Peterson says it in his paraphrase of Romans 12.

> *In this way we are like the various parts of a human body. Each part gets its meaning from the body as a whole, not the other way around. The body we're talking about is Christ's body of chosen people. Each of us finds our meaning and function as a part of his body. But as a chopped-off finger or cut-off toe we wouldn't amount to much, would we? So since we find ourselves fashioned into all these excellently formed and marvelously functioning parts in Christ's body, let's just go ahead and be what we were made to be, without enviously or pridefully comparing ourselves with each other, or trying to be something we aren't* (Romans 12:4–6 MSG).

We find purpose (and meaning) from the body as a whole, not the other way around! That doesn't suggest our individual role isn't powerful, but that power comes from connectivity to the BODY.

"All of you together are Christ's body, and each of you is a part of it."

THE POWER OF OUR GIFTEDNESS IS FOUND WITHIN OUR PURPOSE.

The POWER of our giftedness is found within our PURPOSE.

The entire body of Christ will always function best when God is powerfully at work through our individual GIFTS.

The church (local/global) doesn't need any rogue prophets trying to direct the body from the outside. That's like a dismembered hand trying to adjust and correct the entire human body while detached! Your local church body doesn't need a lone wolf interpreter of tongues (and speaker of tongues) who attaches greater value to their gift than others in their midst with discernment or wisdom.

We need all of them. Everyone. Together. Understanding their gifts and using them with purpose and power within the body of Christ!

It's time to live On Purpose *For* Purpose.

Reflection Questions

1. In what ways have you misunderstood your spiritual gifts in the past? How might these misunderstandings have limited your effectiveness in God's kingdom?
2. Paul emphasizes that God intentionally places each gift within the body exactly where He wants it to be. What does it mean to you personally that your specific gifts were given "on purpose for purpose"?
3. Consider the body analogy Paul uses. Which part of the body do you most identify with based on your gifting? How does this perspective change how you view your role in your local church?
4. What steps can you take this week to better connect your giftedness to the larger body of Christ? Is there a specific ministry or area of service where your gifts could fulfill their divine purpose?
5. Are there any gifts you've been neglecting or diminishing because you didn't understand their purpose? How might acknowledging these gifts change your spiritual journey?

2

ON PURPOSE FOR PURPOSE

I believe that every believer has something supernatural inside of them. We have not just the presence and Spirit of God (as if that wasn't enough already), but also power through the gifts He has given us by His Spirit.

Everyone who has surrendered their life to Christ has the Spirit of God within them (1 Corinthians 3:16). For many, this is a figure of speech or a poetic term used to describe salvation. Most believers simply do not understand what God has given us, and therefore have no idea of the GIFTEDNESS that lies within them.

You may not believe this, but without taking a step towards this promise, you will never be able to live out the strength that has been given to you ON purpose FOR purpose.

What if I told you that God didn't randomly assign you gifts like some cosmic lottery? What if every ability, every talent, every spiritual gift you possess was strategically placed within you with divine intention? This changes everything about how we approach our gifts, doesn't it?

A MIGHTY HERO WITHIN

I love the story of Gideon. For many, viewing the Old Testament as a historical document is a struggle, as some stories seem to be "embellished" or "too good to be true." I'm a firm believer that these were very real people (flawed nonetheless) who were called by God to live extraordinary lives, and we are blessed to have their stories documented.

Gideon was an imperfect hero.

When we meet Gideon, he was living in the time of the Hebrew Judges, and his tribe (family & friends) were frequently invaded and terrorized by foreigners, the Midianites. Without any infrastructure or protection, the Midianite hordes would ride through the region, taking what they wanted, killing whomever they wanted, and leaving nothing but destruction in their wake. When they rode through villages, they were described as being as thick as locusts. The Israelites hid themselves in mountains, caves, and fortified homes in an effort to escape their brutality.

One day, Gideon was down in a winepress threshing wheat (most of us don't have any idea what that means). I'll rephrase. One day, Gideon was down in a pit where they smashed grapes for wine, hiding so no one would see him cutting and threshing wheat so that he and his family could have flour to make bread. The angel of the Lord sat under a tree and began speaking to Gideon.

> *"The angel of the Lord appeared to him and said, 'Mighty hero, the Lord is with you!'"* (Judges 6:12)

What an interesting way to address Gideon, or anyone, for the first time. This encounter was special, but not just because an angel spoke to a man (this happened often throughout the Old Testament). No, this encounter began with a declarative statement about Gideon. Gideon, who was scared to death, was doing all he could to provide food for his family before an enemy could spot him working. He could be robbed or killed over this wheat. "Mighty Hero" wouldn't seem to be an obvious greeting.

Can you imagine how jarring this must have been for Gideon? Picture yourself at your most anxious moment—maybe hiding from a challenge, ducking responsibility, or feeling completely inadequate—and suddenly God's messenger appears and calls you by the very title you feel least qualified to carry. This wasn't just a greeting; it was a divine declaration of Gideon's purpose-filled identity that he had yet to step into.

Gideon responded in a way that makes perfect sense, considering his circumstances. He answered (Judges 6:13) by saying, "*If the Lord is with us, why has all of this happened to us? Where are the miracles? God has abandoned us and given us over to the Midianites.*"

God's response to Gideon was so powerful that I simply don't want to rush past it. Gideon was not wrong, by the way. Earlier in Judges 6, we see that God *had* indeed given the Israelites over to the Midianites. Miracles had ceased, and for all Gideon knew, God had indeed abandoned them.

The first step in finding an answer to a problem is recognizing that there *is* one. That's what Gideon was doing.

However, God wasn't "blown away" by Gideon's accusations. He didn't immediately strike him down with a lightning bolt because Gideon didn't have enough faith. Gideon's journey of faith is one of the reasons I *love* his story. God allowed him to clearly state the problem so that He could provide the solution.

> "*Then the Lord turned to him and said, 'Go with the strength you have, and rescue Israel from the Midianites. I am sending you!*'" (Judges 6:14)

"You're the solution to the problem, Gideon!" I love that God made this crystal clear. "Well done, Gideon! You're correct about the problem, and here's the solution: **it's *you*.**"

GO WITH THE STRENGTH YOU HAVE

There is so much more to Gideon's story that I simply can't get into. I encourage you to read Judges 6–9 if you're interested in learning what happens. I want to spend some time here at the beginning of his story so we can better understand the beginning of *our* story.

Gideon would realize over the course of his journey that He *was* a mighty hero.

Maybe he didn't feel that way at first, but over time, he grew in his faith and trust in God to intercede on his behalf. Gideon had to take baby steps towards his ordained calling by God because he initially struggled to believe that he was indeed a "mighty hero."

God (through the angel) told Gideon to "Go with the strength you have," which, in my opinion, is a powerful phrase. God knew that Gideon would need to grow in his faith and understanding of exactly what God had planned for him. He wanted Gideon to *take the step* that he could take. The one right in front of him that would push the limits of the strength that he already possessed.

That strength within him was given by God. God knew what Gideon was capable of for his first step, just like God also knew what Gideon would look like when the entire Jewish nation would recognize him as a "mighty hero."

This is the divine pattern that teaches us about purpose: *God identifies the gift before we even recognize it in ourselves.* He sees the mighty hero when we're still hiding in the winepress. And He never demands we become fully developed in our purpose overnight—He simply asks us to take the next step with the strength we already have.

The primary challenge of this book is to help you understand that God has already GIFTED you by His Spirit. There is already a strength within you that you may not realize is there.

God doesn't expect us to live out the perfect expression of a GIFTED LIFE on day one of this revelation. He wants us to take the step we can with the power we currently have. The strength that has been placed in us by God Himself ON purpose FOR purpose.

There is already GIFTEDNESS inside every follower of Jesus.

I'm calling that "mighty hero" out of you.

"GIFTED Child of God… the Lord is with *you*!"

BUT, I'M A NOBODY!

Gideon stumbled right out of the gate. God called him to take the step He knew He could, but Gideon couldn't do it without giving God pushback.

> *"But Lord," Gideon replied, "how can I rescue Israel? My clan is the weakest in the whole tribe of Manasseh, and I am the least in my entire family!"* (Judges 6:15)

Gideon went straight to the heart of his deepest insecurities. "I'm a NOBODY! God, not only am I a NOBODY in my entire community of SOMEBODIES, I'm the NOBODY'EST NOBODY in my circle of family and friends."

This might not be the exact phrasing we use when God prompts us, but it's not much different.

Here are just a few modern examples of our excuses to God.

- "Who am I, God, to tell them about You… my life's a wreck!"
- "God, I can't do that. I'm introverted!"
- "God, I'm not sure You've got the right person. Jane's got more faith than I do… ask her!"
- "I've messed up everything else in my life, I'm not going to mess up something that has to do with God."
- "I could never do _____ like Tim does _____, God could never use me like that."
- "Isn't that the pastor's job?"

To be honest, especially in today's western culture, we spend more time telling God why "we can't possibly do (fill in the blank)" than we do studying and believing that *we can do all things through Christ, who gives us strength*!

I remember counseling a young woman who had the most incredible gift of compassion I'd ever witnessed. When I suggested she might consider leading a support group for grieving parents—something our church desperately needed—her immediate response was, "But I don't have a degree in counseling." She couldn't see that her gift wasn't random; it was purposefully placed in her by God for such a time as this. Six months later, after taking that first terrifying step, she was leading a thriving ministry that was healing hearts in ways no textbook training ever could. Her gift had purpose written all over it.

> **WE CAN DO ALL THINGS THROUGH CHRIST, WHO GIVES US STRENGTH!**

I WILL BE WITH YOU

God gave Gideon a very specific answer to his very specific problem. However, He prefaced that answer with a promise repeated over and over throughout the Old and New Testaments.

> *"The Lord said to him, 'I will be with you. And you will destroy the Midianites as if you were fighting against one man'"* (Judges 6:16).

Gideon was called to defeat the enemy. God said, "You will defeat the entire enemy as if you were simply fighting one man." This ties back to the "go in the strength you have" statement God made earlier. He wanted Gideon to know that he would fight and should do all that he could to conquer the enemy, but it would be like the effort required to fight only one man.

God was clearly reassuring Gideon, "I'll take care of the rest of them. You're going to fight, but leave the supernatural, impossible, improbable, and unrealistic part of this plan up to me."

This response is also intended for each of us who is reading Gideon's story. God said, "I will be with you…" This is all we need.

We don't need the full description of "how" our GIFTEDNESS will be used to impact the lives of others.

We don't need to see all the details of how using our GIFTS will transform our lives and the lives of those we touch.

We don't need the timeline of how our GIFTS will grow and strengthen over time.

We simply need to understand that God is with us!

I'm not telling you that growing in your GIFTEDNESS is easy. I'm not saying that it won't be some of the hardest work that you will do in the course of your journey.

So, what am I saying?

I am calling you to tap into the power you already have (given by God) and trust that He is with you as you live ON purpose FOR purpose.

Reflection Questions

1. When have you felt like Gideon, hiding in a "winepress" while God sees you as a "mighty hero"? What gifts might God be calling out in you that you've been hesitant to acknowledge?
2. God told Gideon to "go with the strength you have." What is one step you could take today, using the strength you already have, to begin living out your gifting more purposefully?
3. Which of the excuses listed in this chapter do you most often tell yourself when God prompts you to use your gifts? What truth from Scripture could help you counter this specific excuse?
4. How does understanding that your gifts were given "on purpose FOR purpose" change the way you view your role in God's kingdom work?
5. Gideon needed to hear "I will be with you" before stepping into his calling. In what specific area of using your gifts do you need to trust God's presence more fully? How might remembering His presence with you change your approach to that area?

3

WHAT GIFTS?

This book is designed to help anyone begin to understand and grow in their Spiritual Gifts. There are many resources available on each gift, so don't consider this an exhaustive study. In this chapter, I will provide a simple overview that I will later break down into individual sections, allowing you to study each section separately.

Think of this chapter as your spiritual gifts "orientation"—your first step in discovering what God has placed within you ON purpose FOR purpose. Just like an explorer needs a map before embarking on a journey, you need this overview before diving deeper into your divine design.

WHERE TO BEGIN

It all starts with an assessment. It's like a test, but people tend to dislike tests, so we refer to them as assessments as adults. Most assessments will identify the primary gifts listed in Scripture, with some additional gifts here and there.

If you take an assessment from a Baptist-affiliated organization, you may not get as many questions about the manifestation gifts (tongues, interpretation, prophecy, etc.), and they might have a few additional gifts, such as music.

If you take an assessment from a Pentecostal-affiliated organization, you might get more questions about the manifestation gifts (tongues, interpretation, prophecy, etc), and other auxiliary gifts (like leadership, craftsmanship) will be aligned with how the manifestation gifts are used.

What I'm trying to say is there is no "ideal" Spiritual Gifts test.

I've created a FREE TEST and believe it aligns best with this book, but feel free to go online and find a free or paid one you like.

FREE

I've created The Gifted Purpose Assessment^{IP}, a free test available at **mattdawson.tv/yourspiritualgifts** that's specifically designed to work hand-in-hand with this book. In about 5–10 minutes, it will identify your top 5 spiritual gifts and reveal your primary gift category—whether you're strongest in Motivational, Ministry, or Manifestation gifts. This gives you the exact framework we'll be using throughout the rest of these chapters. The assessment asks 70 targeted questions that cut through the confusion and get straight to how God has wired you. It's completely free because I believe everyone deserves clarity about their spiritual DNA without cost being a barrier.

PAID PRODUCTS

UniquelyYou.org

This is my favorite paid service, offering multiple options. I like that they combine your DISC (personality assessment and identification) profile with your Spiritual Gifts profile to help you better understand how your giftedness works within your personality type. If you just want to take the Spiritual Gifts test, I suggest the "23 Gifts Profile," as it covers all three categories of gifts.

Stop reading and take the assessment now. You will benefit greatly as you complete this chapter.

I mean it—really, stop reading! I've watched too many people skip this step, thinking they'll come back to it later, only to miss the profound clarity that comes when you put a name to what God has placed within you. The assessment isn't magic, but it's an incredible starting point for understanding your purpose. Your gifts weren't randomly assigned; they were intentionally placed in you FOR something specific!

THREE-IN-ONE SPIRITUAL GIFTS

There is debate among theologians as to the premise and purpose of splitting up the GIFTS given to us into three different categories. I don't waste time arguing with theologians who love to argue. The reason I like to split them up is because they were written (by the Holy Spirit through Paul) specifically with words and phrases that not only distinguish the giver of these gifts (God, Jesus, the Holy Spirit) but also their purpose.

The most common titles for these categories are: Motivational Gifts, Ministry Gifts, and Manifestation Gifts, respectively.

SEVEN GIFTS GIVEN BY GOD THE FATHER

> *In His grace, God has given us different gifts for doing certain things well.*
>
> —Romans 12:6

The gifts given to us by God the Father are most commonly known as the Motivational Gifts. They are also referred to as Enabling Gifts, Administrative Gifts, or Aptitude Gifts. Listed in Romans 12:6–8, these characteristics seem to describe the basic motivations or inherent tendencies in a person that align with God's purpose in their initial gifting. Paul writes it in a way that suggests we might "already be doing these things," so we should do them with the understanding that God has gifted you in this way.

These gifts are: **Prophecy, Serving Others (Helps), Teaching, Giving, Encouragement, Leadership,** and **Mercy.**

> *...so if God has given you the ability to prophesy, speak out with as much faith as God has given you. If your gift is serving others, serve them well. If you are a teacher, teach well. If your gift is to encourage others, be encouraging. If it is giving, give generously. If God has given you leadership ability, take the responsibility seriously. And if you have a gift for showing kindness to others, do it gladly* (Romans 12:6–8).

Notice something profound here? God doesn't just tell you *what* your gift is, but *how* to use it. This isn't a casual suggestion; it's divine direction. If you have the gift of encouragement, God doesn't just say "be encouraging" but implies "be *intentionally* encouraging because that's part of your PURPOSE." Each gift listed here comes with built-in instructions for purposeful living!

FIVE GIFTS GIVEN BY JESUS CHRIST

> *There is one Lord, one faith, one baptism, one God and Father of all, who is over all, in all, and living through all. However, he has given each one of us a special gift through the generosity of Christ.*
>
> —Ephesians 4:5–7

The gifts given to us by Jesus Christ are most commonly known as the Ministry Gifts. They are also referred to as Office Gifts, Equipping Gifts, or Team Gifts. Listed in Ephesians 4:11–12, they are stated with a specific purpose. Jesus gave these gifts "to the church." We believe Paul was referring to the original word Jesus used for church—ecclesia (movement, gathering)—and does not refer to the organization or your local church, but rather to the entire body of Christ. They are also described in further detail in verse 12, where it is stated that they are to be used "to equip God's people (the Church) to do His work, and build up the church, the body of Christ."

These gifts are: **Apostle, Prophet, Shepherd (Pastor), Teacher,** and **Evangelist.**

> *"Now these are the gifts Christ gave to the church: the apostles, the prophets, the evangelists, and the pastors and teachers. Their responsibility is to equip God's people to do his work and build up the church, the body of Christ"* (Ephesians 4:11–12).

I've seen far too many believers dismiss these gifts as only belonging to those with formal titles or positions. But what if that's a fundamental misunderstanding of Jesus' purpose?

What if being an evangelist isn't just for those with "Evangelist" on their business cards, but for anyone God has given this gift to? These gifts weren't given to create hierarchies *but to fulfill a purpose.* Your gift might be pastoral in nature even if you've never stood behind a pulpit in your life. Understanding these gifts helps you see how Jesus strategically placed certain abilities within you for His kingdom purposes.

NINE GIFTS GIVEN BY THE HOLY SPIRIT

> *There are different kinds of spiritual gifts, but the same Spirit is the source of them all. There are different kinds of service, but we serve the same Lord. God works in different ways, but it is the same God who does the work in all of us. A spiritual gift is given to each of us so we can help each other.*
>
> —1 Corinthians 12:4–7

More has been written about gifts given by the Holy Spirit than the other two categories combined. Many groups and denominations believe that the "speaking gifts" were only temporarily given to the first-century church to help them establish churches around the world. Others believe these gifts are a primary expression of the Holy Spirit indwelling a person (second Baptism). I will go into greater detail about each gift later in this book, but for now, here is a summary.

The gifts given to us by the Holy Spirit are most commonly known as the Manifestation Gifts. They are also referred to as Miraculous Gifts, Edifying Gifts, or Operational Gifts. Listed in 1 Corinthians 12:8–10, these gifts seem to reveal the supernatural power of God in our lives. Although all gifts are supernaturally given (John 3:6 "The Holy Spirit gives birth to spiritual life"), these nine gifts display the supernatural power of God within us. The stated purpose is given in verse 7: "These gifts are given to each of us so we can help each other," which indicates that the primary use of these gifts is to benefit the body of the church. Paul instructed in verse 31 that "we should earnestly desire the most helpful gifts." Paul also addressed specific gifts in 1 Corinthians 14, describing some as external gifts (to reveal God to unbelievers) and others as internal (to bring a message to believers).

These gifts are: **Wisdom, Special Knowledge, Faith, Healing, Miracles, Prophecy, Distinguishing Between Spirits (Discernment), Tongues,** and **Interpretation of Tongues.**

> *To one person the Spirit gives the ability to give wise advice; to another the same Spirit gives a message of special knowledge. The same Spirit gives great faith to another, and to someone else the one Spirit gives the gift of healing. He gives one person the power to perform miracles, and another the ability to prophesy. He gives someone else the ability to discern whether a message is from the Spirit of God or from another spirit. Still another person is given the ability to speak in unknown languages, while another is given the ability to interpret what is being said* (1 Corinthians 12:8–10).

I've witnessed firsthand how these gifts become divisive in church communities when they should be unifying. Some churches elevate them to exclusive status while others dismiss them entirely. But what if both approaches miss the point? These gifts weren't given for theological battlegrounds *but for purposeful kingdom work.* Whether you believe all these gifts are for today or not, the essential truth remains: there is a Gifted DNA Blueprint[IP] for each of us. The Holy Spirit gives specific abilities to specific people for specific purposes. Your spiritual DNA contains exactly what the body of Christ needs at this moment in history.

ADDITIONAL GIFTS

There are four additional gifts that seem to overlap in meaning and title and are sometimes listed within these three categories. However, I will list them separately since there are several other passages that refer to them.

These gifts are: **Hospitality, Intercession, Administration,** and **Craftsmanship.**[1]

- **Hospitality References:** Acts 16:14–15; Romans 12:13, 16:23; Hebrews 13:1–2; 1 Peter 4:9
- **Intercession References:** Hebrews 7:25; Colossians 1:9–12, 4:12–13; James 5:14–16
- **Administration References:** Luke 14:28–30; Acts 6:1–7; 1 Corinthians 12:28
- **Craftsmanship References:** Exodus 30:22, 31:3–11; 2 Chronicles 34:9–13; Acts 18:2–3

These "additional" gifts sometimes get overlooked in our discussions, yet they're profoundly important to the functioning of God's kingdom. I knew a woman whose gift of hospitality transformed our church community more deeply than many of our teaching programs. Never minimize a gift because it seems ordinary—remember that in God's economy, the "ordinary" is often where the most extraordinary work happens. These gifts aren't afterthoughts; they're *essential elements* of God's purposeful design.

GIFTS OR TALENTS?

One question that emerges when doing a spiritual gifts study is the distinction between a GIFT and a TALENT. There are other resources you can use to explore the world that align with and separate these two characteristics, but I will give you the baseline apologetic we will assume for this book.

TALENTS

Talents are given to us by God and strengthened by our willingness to exercise and perfect them. There are no shortages on the list of talents that God has given us as a human species.

One of my favorite YouTube guilty pleasures is watching Dude Perfect videos. These are the young men who throw tennis balls and footballs off of skyscrapers, through a maze of hoola-hoops, all to land perfectly through a basketball net set up so far away they can barely see it. I know that it's not impossible, but every trick they do is so improbable that I end up losing 2 hours in a black hole of endless videos. This is a TALENT.

I'm sure you've seen many people do what seems impossible to most of us, but they make it look so easy. Some have a talent for math, while others have a talent for connecting strangers over a business lunch. Some are physical talents, like those in sports (Michael Jordan, Babe Ruth), and others are intellectual (Stephen Hawking, Albert Einstein). Some are artistic (Jimi Hendrix, Whitney Houston), while others are seen as more entertaining (Stephen King, Julia Roberts).

No matter the talent, the path is almost always the same. People are born with a bent and an aptitude that is discovered early in life. They spend time exercising this talent, developing it, and some even perfect it.

The primary distinction that makes a talent different from a spiritual gift is that although both are given to us by our Creator, a talent does not require the indwelling of the Holy Spirit in our lives.

Many people granted talents by God do not recognize, serve, or even want to know God. That does not diminish their talents or hinder their growth. Talents are inherent abilities provided by the Creator of life (Psalms 139:14). *"Thank You for making me so wonderfully complex! Your workmanship is marvelous—how well I know it."*

SPIRITUAL GIFTS

Spiritual Gifts are given to us by God. Jesus told Nicodemus that the process of being "born again" was not a physical rebirth but a spiritual rebirth (John 3:1–8). Paul tells us that when we receive Christ as our Savior, we die to this life and our real life becomes hidden with Christ in God (Colossians 3:3). That new life in us is guided by the Holy Spirit that lives in us and produces "fruit" in us (Galatians 5:22–23).

Spiritual gifts are supernaturally given when we receive our *new life* through Jesus Christ. That is what distinguishes our GIFTEDNESS.

I wish that because of my salvation and the indwelling of the Holy Spirit, I could all of a sudden become a professional basketball player! That's not going to happen. That's not the purpose of our spiritual gifts. Talents can be fueled and encouraged by our spiritual gifts, but they do not arrive in our lives because of a spiritual rebirth.

> SPIRITUAL GIFTS ARE GIVEN TO US FOR PURPOSE, TRANSFORMATION, AND TO HAVE AN IMPACT FOR THE KINGDOM OF GOD.

Spiritual Gifts are given to us for purpose, transformation, and to have an impact for the kingdom of God. They are not a list of things we can achieve based on how much faith we have or how hard we work for Christ. These gifts are given in variety, and God alone decides who is granted which gifts. 1 Corinthians 12:11 *"It is the one and only Spirit who distributes all these gifts. He alone decides which gift each person should have."*

Here's a perspective that transformed my understanding: What if your talents are the delivery system for your spiritual gifts? Think about it—God doesn't waste anything. If you're naturally talented at communication and spiritually gifted in encouragement, that's no coincidence. That's divine engineering! I've seen this with musicians who are technically talented, but when combined with their spiritual gift of prophecy, their music becomes a vehicle for God's voice to reach places logic never could. Your talents and gifts aren't competing categories; they're complementary tools, strategically combined by God for maximum kingdom impact. This is called the Gifted DNA Blueprint.

WHAT ABOUT THE FRUIT OF THE SPIRIT?

Everyone who receives Christ as their Savior will see the evidence of the Holy Spirit in their lives through the FRUIT mentioned in Galatians 5:22–23: Love, Joy, Peace, Patience, Kindness, Goodness, Faithfulness, Gentleness, and Self-Control. These are not talents *or* spiritual gifts. These are characteristics that should mark every follower of Christ as evidence that the Holy Spirit is doing a work in their lives.

The Fruit of the Spirit is the product of a life surrendered to the leadership, guidance, and will of the Holy Spirit and should *all* be evident in our lives (even if in varying degrees).

Think of it this way: spiritual gifts are what you *do*, while the fruit of the Spirit is who you *are*. A spiritually gifted person without fruit is like a powerful car without a driver—impressive but dangerous.

The most gifted teacher who lacks patience and kindness becomes a spiritual liability rather than an asset. Your gifts fulfill God's purpose through your actions, while the fruit fulfills God's purpose through your character. Both are essential parts of living ON purpose FOR purpose.

WHY GIFTS?

Over the next several chapters, I want to spend time addressing why we have been GIFTED before we dig into the Gifted Gifts Codex^{IP}. Hopefully, you've already taken the assessment and have a fundamental understanding of how you have been gifted.

However, this book is also a tool. If you would like a deeper understanding of your primary gifts before exploring why you've been gifted with them, refer to Chapters 7 through 9 and then return after gaining a better understanding of your individual giftedness.

The goal is to help you live ON Purpose FOR Purpose by learning your gift mix and understanding how to utilize the supernatural power of God in your life by using your spiritual gifts!

> ### Reflection Questions
>
> 1. What was your reaction to your top spiritual gifts after taking the assessment? Were you surprised, confused, or did it confirm what you already suspected about yourself?
> 2. How might understanding the difference between talents and spiritual gifts change the way you view abilities you've taken for granted or dismissed as "just who you are"?

3. Which category of gifts (Motivational, Ministry, or Manifestation) feels most natural to you, and which feels most challenging to understand or accept? Why do you think that is?

4. In what specific ways could your spiritual gifts complement your natural talents to fulfill God's purpose for your life? Can you identify any "divine engineering" in how these work together?

5. What steps will you take this week to intentionally use one of your spiritual gifts in a way that serves others and advances God's kingdom? How might this step move you closer to living "on purpose FOR purpose"?

4

THE MEANING AND PURPOSE OF LIFE

> *The meaning of life is to find your gift.*
> *The purpose of life is to give it away.*
> —David Viscott, psychiatrist and author

When I first considered writing a resource to empower people in their spiritual gifts, I couldn't shake the dynamic potential of you and me waking up to the purpose of our lives. Our individual gifts were not simply given to us randomly (like the spinning of the bingo ball cage) but rather distributed ON purpose and FOR purpose! Once we understand that we've been gifted for a purpose, it has the potential to change the trajectory of our lives. It shifts us from floating aimlessly in an ocean of possibilities to following a steadfast course, utilizing all we've been granted to fuel us on our journey.

Think about that for a moment. What if nothing about your spiritual makeup is accidental? What if those unique abilities that come so naturally to you—the ones that make your friends say "how do you do that?"—were intentionally planted within you by the Creator of the universe with a specific kingdom purpose in mind? That's not just encouraging—that's life-altering!

WHY AM I HERE?

This is the primary question that most of us ask when it comes to the purpose of life.

Some answers might include: pursuing a career, raising a family, engaging in mission work, simply loving people, enjoying life, embracing the philosophy of "carpe diem," loving God, achieving significant milestones, making the world a better place, and leaving this world in a better state than we found it.

These are not bad things to do. Some of these are good and necessary (like loving God, raising families, and working), but they don't provide an answer to the question. They cannot reach the depth of a person's soul as they contemplate their existence on this earth!

Many people then look for "spiritual" answers to this question. Buddhists believe the purpose of life is to end suffering. Evangelical Christians will say it's about loving God and loving others. Catholics say it is to serve God and the Church. Humanists believe that man's effort creates life's meaning. Evolutionists believe life's purpose is to continue evolving. Muslims believe man's purpose is to worship Allah. And many atheists believe that they are solely responsible for creating meaning in life.

Since the answers to this question seem to be whatever one wants them to be, it's no wonder that so many people struggle to find fulfillment and satisfaction in their lives. It doesn't really matter how practical or spiritual we choose to be; if we think the purpose of life is a secret, we will wander from philosophy to philosophy looking for someone with a clue to discover it!

ON PURPOSE, FOR PURPOSE

I was 26 years old when I first visited a Presbyterian church that friends had invited me to. I was an active volunteer at another church, but my wife and I were very unhappy with its culture and had begun searching for a new place to call home. I don't recall the first time I heard of the Westminster Catechisms, but I remember someone reading the first question during worship at that Presbyterian church one day. I remember seeing it projected on a large screen and its unforgettable message:

> *"What is the chief end of man? To glorify God and enjoy Him forever!"*[2]

I remember agreeing with this statement, but I also appreciated the fact that they had put "enjoy" in it. One of our struggles in our former church culture was the lack of everyday joy. We had plenty to be joyful about for eternity; however, it was overshadowed by an everyday life of written and unwritten rules for Christians in our fallen world.

I had never considered that "enjoying" God was connected to my purpose in life! For a list of reasons too long to explain, I had come to believe that what I enjoyed was probably some variation of sin, and therefore God would be angry and send me to the back of the line of His favor and blessing. You may not have struggled with this, but that was a big deal for me as a young adult.

I remember the freedom I felt that day—like chains falling away from my understanding of God. What if the things I was naturally good at, the activities that made me lose track of time, weren't spiritual distractions but divine indicators? What if God had wired me to enjoy certain things because those very things were pathways to fulfilling my purpose? This paradigm shift changed everything for me.

I've spent the last 25 years helping convince Christians that God has a purpose for our lives and that we actually get to ENJOY that life. When we position our lives to GLORIFY Him (honor, love, serve, give, sacrifice), we get to ENJOY Him.

Jesus said it this way when giving instructions on everyday life (money, possessions, relationships, fear, worry):

> *"Don't store up treasures here on earth, where moths eat them and rust destroys them, and where thieves break in and steal. Store your treasures in heaven, where moths and rust cannot destroy, and thieves do not break in and steal. Wherever your treasure is, there the desires of your heart will also be"* (Matthew 6:19–21).

Jesus taught that enjoying life was not driven by hoarding material possessions that are here today and gone tomorrow, but about investing in the bigger picture. The eternal connection that aligns our hearts for purpose and fulfillment is tied to what we treasure most.

WE WERE CREATED ON PURPOSE, FOR PURPOSE.

This is the "key," if you will, to unlocking the hidden purpose of your life. Once we recognize that we were created to glorify God and enjoy Him forever (for Purpose), we must begin the process of seeing how He has uniquely gifted us (on Purpose) to do so.

> *Now may the God of peace—who brought up from the dead our Lord Jesus, the great Shepherd of the sheep, and ratified an eternal covenant with his blood— may he equip you with all you need for doing his will. May he produce in you, through the*

power of Jesus Christ, every good thing that is pleasing to him. All glory to him forever and ever! Amen (Hebrews 13:20–21).

God equips us by giving spiritual gifts to be used to glorify Him. In this way, He will produce in us, through the power of Jesus Christ, every good thing that is pleasing to him! This is how we glorify God.

The Apostle Paul tells us that "God has given each of you a gift from his great variety of spiritual gifts. Use them well to serve one another" (1 Peter 4:10). This is one of the primary ways we glorify God. We SERVE one another using the gifts that God has given us.

At Journey Church, where I serve as Lead Pastor, we state that one of the "Core Ambitions" of a follower of Jesus is Serving.[3] Why? Because we believe that "Serving Brings Purpose!" Nothing reveals and allows us to live out our God-given purpose more than sacrificially serving one another.

Some are given the spiritual gift of SERVING (*Romans 12:7 "If your gift is serving others, serve them well…"*). However, we all serve each other when we work on our giftedness. If you LEAD, take that responsibility seriously and lead others well. If you PROPHESY, speak out with as much faith as God has given you! One who prophesies encourages, comforts, and strengthens others (1 Corinthians 14:3). If your gift is to ENCOURAGE others, be the greatest cheerleader you can be! If your gift is GIVING, then create as many opportunities to be generous as you can. Don't wait for them to come to you - find ways to serve others by GIVING. Those with a gift of WISDOM serve others by example and by teaching. I could go on and on.

We not only get to glorify God when living out of our giftedness, but we also get to ENJOY HIM by experiencing the fullness of our individual purposes.

WHERE WE LIVE, WORK, AND PLAY

Many assume that because we are gifted to serve one another, be helpful, and build up the church (Romans 12; 1 Corinthians 12; Ephesians 4), our gifts are *only* used on Sunday mornings, our weekly Bible study group, and maybe on a mission trip. This is one of the reasons most do not LIVE OUT the STRENGTH they have in their lives: they have reduced the use of GIFTS to "church activities."

I've watched many believers compartmentalize their spiritual gifts, as though God only works between 9 and 12 on Sunday mornings. But what if the teacher who instructs with clarity on Sunday is meant to bring that same gift into her corporate training role on Tuesday? What if the man with the gift of encouragement isn't meant just to greet people at the church doors but to transform his sales team's culture? Your gifts weren't designed to be confined to church buildings—they were meant to influence every domain of your life.

God did not exclusively see organized church programs as the "life" He called you to. To glorify God and enjoy Him forever applies to EVERY area of our lives. I like the phrase "where we live, work, and play." This encompasses everything: school, job, home, hobbies, family, vacations, church, travel, rest, and celebration!

I recently asked people from my church how they saw their spiritual gifts being used in their daily lives, whether at work, at play, or in their community. Here are some great responses from partners at Journey (their primary gifts are highlighted).

> "In my daily life at work, home, and church life, I enjoy **encouraging** others with prayer and teaching about how God's grace has the power to bring hope in any situation! Encouraging people is my natural desire and response wherever I am!" —SN

"I worked as a **teacher** in preschool for over 20 years. I felt like I was good at that because God gave me ways to explain things, whether academic or Christian, in basic, simple ways" —SD

"I think one way that I see **discernment** expressed regularly is in listening to people and truly processing with them. I can't tell you how many times I've encountered people who are just desperate for someone to listen to them and work through stuff with someone else. Oftentimes, a different perspective is all they need, and it's incredible to watch how God can use a simple insight to change their view, outlook, or even attitude towards a situation or challenge." —CD

"At work, I use **discernment** and **words of knowledge** all the time when working with people in emotional and/or spiritual sessions to help lead them to root issues. Several times, I've heard the Holy Spirit speak during a session with a client about a certain relationship in their life, or He will highlight certain parts of my conversations with them to help me pinpoint where we need to focus. I love that I get to lay hands on and pray for **healing** over people's physical bodies, their emotions, and their spiritual life frequently. Many times, I will pray in **tongues** over someone, and I will get an **interpretation** in my spirit of specifically how the spirit was praying through me for them." —BK

"The gift of **administration** helps me see how to break down a potentially overwhelming task into a series of discrete categories and then further into discrete tasks that make the work more manageable. When working in my area of primary gifting, there is an ease, a sense of rightness that comes from living out your potential, of a job truly well done." —LT

"**Faith** shows up at work as well. With every phone call I make... I pray first. Before a planning meeting... I pray first. When sending out emails... I pray for the right words. When I'm operating within my gifted areas, I feel like I'm In The Zone—Playing In The Pocket!" —CW

If the Holy Spirit indwells us 24/7, I can't imagine that God's sole purpose for our spiritual gifts is limited to some use on Sunday. However, many Christians assume this.

The truth is that we can always be in Gifted Everywhere Ministry Mode[IP]. God has gifted you ON purpose FOR purpose where you live, work, and play!

TO DO OR TO BE?

When we embark on a journey of purpose, it's easy to get caught up in a list of what we are supposed to DO—believing that with purpose comes accomplishment or some big goal that stretches us to shoot for the stars. Christians and non-Christians alike will quickly trade their eternal purpose for a list of short- and long-term goals that can be easily translated into behaviors.

Think about it—when someone asks about your purpose, how quickly do your thoughts drift to *achievements*, *activities*, or *accomplishments*? "I'm supposed to build a ministry," or "I'm called to write a book," or "I'm meant to help people through counseling." These are all wonderful things, but they're the WHAT, not the WHO of your purpose.

However, living ON purpose FOR purpose by living out of our giftedness is not about what we do; it's about who we are! Who we are determines what we do and how we do it, but that is not the same as our purpose. Our purpose is to BE who GOD GIFTED US TO BE! That is why Paul used the visual illustration of the human body (1 Corinthians 12:14–21).

Your spiritual gift is not the detailed list of "what the hand does," it is being the HAND He's calling you to be. It's WHO YOU ARE as you are connected to the body. Don't miss how he stated the gifts that God has given.

> *Just as our bodies have many parts and each part has a special function, so it is with Christ's body. We are many parts of one body, and we all belong to each other. In his grace, God has given us different gifts for doing certain things well. So if God has given you the ability to prophesy, speak out with as much faith as God has given you. If your gift is serving others, serve them well. If you are a teacher, teach well. If your gift is to encourage others, be encouraging. If it is giving, give generously. If God has given you leadership ability, take the responsibility seriously. And if you have a gift for showing kindness to others, do it gladly* (Romans 12:4–8).

> *"Now these are the gifts Christ gave to the church: the apostles, the prophets, the evangelists, and the pastors and teachers"* (Ephesians 4:11).

> *To one person the Spirit gives the ability to give wise advice; to another the same Spirit gives a message of special knowledge. The same Spirit gives great faith to another, and to someone else the one Spirit gives the gift of healing. He gives one person the power to perform miracles, and another the ability to prophesy. He gives someone else the ability to discern whether a message is from the Spirit of God or from another spirit. Still another person is given the ability to speak in unknown languages, while another is given the ability to interpret what is being said* (1 Corinthians 12:8–10).

> *"The human body has many parts, but the many parts make up one whole body. So it is with the body of Christ"* (1 Corinthians 12:12).

Yes, the body has many different parts, not just one part. If the foot says, "I am not a part of the body because I am not a hand," that does not make it any less a part of the body. And if the ear says, "I am not part of the body because I am not an eye," would that make it any less a part of the body? If the whole body were an eye, how would you hear? Or if your whole body were an ear, how would you smell anything? But our bodies have many parts, and God has put each part just where he wants it. How strange a body would be if it had only one part! Yes, there are many parts, but only one body. The eye can never say to the hand, "I don't need you." The head can't say to the feet, "I don't need you" (1 Corinthians 12:14–21).

The action of the gifts detailed is given as an example, not as a list or command of what to do. It's an example of "who" we are as it relates to the body (bigger picture).

The action list is not your PURPOSE.

Being who God has called you to be and living out of your GIFTS is what you were created for! *That is your Purpose.*

THE GIFTED DISTRACTION DETECTION SYSTEM[IP]

Growing in your spiritual giftedness requires focus and intention. In a world filled with technological and recreational noise, it takes little time for us to get distracted.

I'm distracted right now, writing this book. I would rather be headed somewhere with someone to do something we both enjoy, or simply binge-watching the latest popular show on Netflix. Don't lie. You'd rather be doing that than reading this book as well—I know you!

PSST....That notification just buzzed on your phone, didn't it? And part of you is wondering if you should check it before finishing this paragraph. We live in the age of unprecedented distraction, where everything is engineered to pull our attention away from purpose and toward pleasure, convenience, or urgent-but-not-important matters.

Distractions tell us that "there's a better, easier way to get what you want."

Nothing tempts our fallen nature like a well-timed, perfectly placed distraction.

> **NOTHING TEMPTS OUR FALLEN NATURE LIKE A WELL-TIMED, PERFECTLY PLACED DISTRACTION.**

Distractions show up at home, at work, with friends, in our cars, on the bus, in the park, at a ball game, in our quiet time, in a crowd of people, or in a place of solitude. Most of us carry around a four-inch screen that is the only interference our Enemy needs to keep us distracted from our giftedness.

The writer of Hebrews reminded readers to throw off the sin that easily trips us up (entangles) and the weight that slows us down; I believe this applies to distractions as well.

> *"Therefore, since we are surrounded by such a huge crowd of witnesses to the life of faith, let us strip off every weight that slows us down, especially the sin that so easily trips us up. And let us run with endurance the race God has set before us. We do this by keeping our eyes on Jesus, the champion who initiates and perfects our faith"* (Hebrews 12:1–2).

Nothing weighs us down more than the assumption that WHAT we do matters more than WHO we are. And we frequently stumble because of distractions that tell us there's a better, easier way to get what we want.

The answer to our purpose is given when our eyes are FIXED on Jesus, the author and perfecter of our faith.

GOD GIVES US A COMPASS, NOT A MAP

Why do we need to keep our "eyes fixed on Jesus?" Because we are all outcome-oriented people. The destination is what matters to most people, not the journey itself. We all want to know where we are going and, more importantly, how things are going to turn out. How we get there is often low on the list of our priorities.

However, once we understand that WHO WE ARE directs and influences what we do and how we live in our giftedness, we can then understand why God gives us a compass, not a map.

This is where we encounter the Compass Navigation Method[IP].

Maps are comfortable. They show every turn, every landmark, every mile marker along the way. But maps become outdated. Detours happen. Construction requires new routes. God doesn't give us the security of a detailed map because He knows the terrain of our lives will change. Instead, He gives us something far more valuable—a compass called the Holy Spirit that always points true north regardless of the shifting landscape around us.

We're not given a map with a big "X" to mark our destination. We don't get the kind of guaranteed outcomes that our minds are searching for. Our purpose in living out our spiritual gifts is aligned with our journey, and not the destination. God has promised to never leave you or forsake you on this journey. It's about who we are becoming, not where we are going or how we'll feel when we get there.

The compass we have been given is the Holy Spirit. He is the one who directs us towards our purpose. He uses our GIFTS to reveal that purpose to us and to help us experience the LIFE that Jesus brings to every believer. Not just life, but a right and satisfying life that Jesus called "life to the full" (John 10:10).

As long as we trust in the Holy Spirit to guide us, we will live each day with purpose.

We may not fully understand all that God is doing in and through us, but we will get to experience the fullness of God as we live ON purpose FOR purpose.

> *I pray that from his glorious, unlimited resources he will empower you with inner strength through his Spirit. Then Christ will make his home in your hearts as you trust in him. Your roots will grow down into God's love and keep you strong. And may you have the power to understand, as all God's people should, how wide, how long, how high, and how deep his love is. May you experience the love of Christ, though it is too great to understand fully. Then you will be made complete with all the fullness of life and power that comes from God* (Ephesians 3:16–19).

I love those encouraging words from Paul. That we can experience how wide, long, high, and deep the love of God is. It's too great to fully understand, but we will be made complete in the fullness of life and power that comes from God.

> *"Now to him who is able to do immeasurably more than all we ask or imagine, according to his power that is at work within us, to him be glory in the church and in Christ Jesus throughout all generations, for ever and ever! Amen"* (Ephesians 3:20–21).

Our purpose is to "glorify God and enjoy Him forever."

We've been gifted on purpose, for purpose. Our gifts are not a list of goals to accomplish, but are who we are becoming. Our purpose is revealed through our individual roles within the larger body of Christ.

Don't get distracted!
Live Your Life ON Purpose FOR Purpose!

Reflection Questions

1. When you consider that your gifts were placed in you "ON purpose FOR purpose," how does that change the way you view your natural abilities and spiritual gifts? What new significance do they take on?

2. What areas of your life (work, home, relationships, hobbies) have you been treating as "gift-free zones" where you haven't been intentionally using your spiritual gifts? How might your purpose express itself in these areas?

3. Think about a time when you felt most "in the zone" or deeply satisfied while serving others. What spiritual gifts were you expressing in that moment? How was that experience connected to both glorifying God and enjoying Him?

4. What specific distractions most commonly pull you away from living in your giftedness? What practical steps could you take this week to minimize these distractions?

5. If you were to embrace the compass (Holy Spirit) rather than demanding a map for your life, what would change about how you make decisions regarding your gifts and calling? How would "who you are" take priority over "what you do"?

5

GIFTED FOR TRANSFORMATION

Once we understand and believe that we have been supernaturally gifted and that those gifts have purpose, we will begin to experience personal transformation. I like the word transformation. It illustrates the complete picture of what actually takes place when we are given a new life in Christ. We do change, evolve, grow, and improve, but these individual attributes don't fully capture the essence of what transformation accomplishes.

Our lives don't simply improve; they transform! We are not the same person we once were when we began living out of our spiritual gifts!

Think about the caterpillar's journey to becoming a butterfly. It's not just about growing bigger or stronger; it's about becoming an entirely different creature with new capabilities and a completely new way of moving through the world. This is what happens when we embrace our spiritual gifts and begin living on purpose FOR purpose!

We are transformed by Christ in an instant, yet it takes a lifetime to mature. We're justified and made righteous at the moment of salvation, but we are sanctified by transforming more and more into the image of Christ each day. We're given every promise up front and realize their fulfillment more and more as we grow in our knowledge and understanding of God.

We are gifted the moment the Holy Spirit takes up residence in our hearts, but transformation results from renewing our minds daily!

CHANGING OUR MINDS

> *Don't copy the behavior and customs of this world, but let God transform you into a new person by changing the way you think. Then you will learn to know God's will for you, which is good and pleasing and perfect.*
>
> —Romans 12:2

Transformation starts in the mind. Our thoughts determine our actions, so when our pattern of thinking changes, what we believe changes. When what we believe (faith) changes, our actions change, and therefore, our lives change. That's transformation!

However, changing how we think is one of the most difficult tasks known to man. This is why we have psychologists and psychiatrists on speed dial. From limiting beliefs to OCD, to battling ADHD, we have accepted that changing the way we think is almost impossible without years of therapy. Don't get me wrong, there are very real issues that many face, and I support getting professional help when necessary. However, our culture has created a gap in understanding transformation because of two extremes: it's either really easy (mind over matter, just do it) or a mental Mount Everest (you may need years of professional help).

I think many Christians who desire transformation in their lives are hoping that it's either easy (Jesus does all the work) or impossible. Real transformation is not a change in how we feel or a larger measure of faith. Transformation happens when we renew our minds and allow them to change our behavior.

"Since you have heard about Jesus and have learned the truth that comes from him, throw off your old sinful nature and your former way of life, which is corrupted by lust and deception. Instead, let the Spirit renew your thoughts and attitudes" (Ephesians 4:21–23).

Have you ever tried to unlearn something? It's incredibly difficult. The neural pathways in our brains become like well-worn hiking trails after years of repetitive thoughts. Retraining our minds to think according to God's truth rather than our old patterns requires intentional effort. But here's the good news: when we align our thinking with how God designed us to function within our giftedness, transformation accelerates dramatically. It's like finally using a tool for its intended purpose rather than forcing it to do a job it wasn't designed for.

FALSE TRANSFORMATION

Since experiencing lasting change is so strenuous (especially when we realize our thought patterns can be habitual and don't change easily), many opt for what "appears" to be a transformed life, only to be disappointed when they don't see any lasting change. When change doesn't last, we assume that either God is not faithful or that we are simply not good enough at this "Christian thing." False transformation is a problem for many believers.

I call these the False Transformation Trilogy[IP].

CONFORMING

To conform is to adapt or apply an expected behavior to our lives. "I should be nice to people, and I've seen a few people be nice. I'll just do that. I can learn all those religious terms; that's easy. What does faith look like? I've seen people do things and then say 'I'm just trusting God with the outcome,' so I'll just add that to my list of things to do." There's also a big list of don'ts. "Don't drink, smoke, or chew . . . or date girls who do." Check!

From the outside looking in, we understand that conforming is not *real* change. It's just modifying our behavior to a new set of guidelines. It's like taking a ratty old couch and putting a fancy new cover on it. The exterior may look a bit different, but the couch beneath remains the same.

I remember coaching a young man who could quote Scripture like a seminary professor and had all the right Christian behaviors—he attended every service, volunteered consistently, and never missed a prayer meeting. But when life hit him hard, all that conformity crumbled because it wasn't anchored in genuine transformation. His gifts remained dormant because he was too busy maintaining an acceptable Christian appearance to discover how God had purposefully designed him to serve.

COMPARING

To transform by comparison is probably the easiest shortcut people take. It's simply viewing the way we look (or the way our actions look) by contrasting them with others' actions. It's not an actual transformation, but depending on who we compare ourselves to, we often appear much better because we have chosen an imperfect standard.

There's no win in comparison.

—Andy Stanley

Finding people to compare our lives to is a hopeless and meaningless endeavor. We can't base our own spiritual growth on overt comparisons with others.

CONDEMNING

Witnessing change propelled by condemnation is one of the most disheartening aspects of behavioral modification. We allow guilt and shame over our current actions and way of thinking to condemn us spiritually (the Enemy loves playing this game with us). Out of this condemnation, our actions may change, but not for the better. Now we just live our lives out of fear and shame. Even if we find ourselves "doing the right things," we are not growing in our faith and walk with Jesus because we're doing them for the wrong reasons. "But whoever has doubts is condemned if they eat, because their eating is not from faith; and everything that does not come from faith is sin" (Romans 14:23).

There are too many followers of Jesus who are trapped in a life of condemnation. They long for transformation, but they need freedom from their thoughts first!

> *"So now there is no condemnation for those who belong to Christ Jesus. And because you belong to him, the power of the life-giving Spirit has freed you from the power of sin that leads to death"* (Romans 8:1–2).

OUR GIFTS TRANSFORM US

When we receive this new life in Jesus Christ, the Holy Spirit gives us a variety of gifts. The work of transformation belongs to Jesus as He helps us renew our minds with our eyes fixed on Him.

When we realize that we have been gifted ON purpose FOR purpose, our job is to grow in our understanding (mind) and exercise (strength) of those gifts by the power of His Spirit. It is a constant flow of God pouring into us as we explore, understand, and apply our individual gifts and use them to strengthen the body of Christ.

When false transformation is rooted in our lives, we cannot grow in our gifts. Why? Because we are stuck in a pattern of relying on our own power and not the power within us (through the Holy Spirit) to accomplish our purposes. When we begin to rely on the Holy Spirit through the use of our gifts, we are sure to grow and see transformation in our lives.

GIFTS IN REAL LIFE

Administration, Faith, and Leadership. It's easy to find ourselves working out of our own strength. Tirelessly, we try to manage everyone and everything. We profess faith but are secretly overwhelmed by fear, and our leadership does not empower others to succeed but siphons their strength to help us stay afloat.

However, when *relying on God's strength* to work in and through us, administration will work in unity with the gifts of others. We are not only driven by faith but see God continually move and work in ways that strengthen our faith (even though fear is still present). When leading, we can empower others to win, celebrating their growth and success without feeling jealous or insecure about our own position. When we live out of our gifts (given to us by the Holy Spirit), our gifts transform us.

I witnessed this transformation in a business leader in our church who had the gift of administration. For years, she ran her department with iron-fisted control, creating impressive results but leaving a trail of burned-out employees. When she began to understand that her gift was given ON purpose FOR purpose, she started to see her role differently. Instead of using her administrative abilities to control outcomes, she began using them to *create systems that allowed others to thrive*. The transformation was remarkable—not just in her department's culture but in her own joy and peace.

Mercy, Exhortation, Hospitality. When we work in our own strength, we have limits on how much we can care for others. We inevitably experience what is called "compassion fatigue." We can lift others up only as long as we ourselves are in a good place mentally and emotionally. We desire to serve and love others well, but again, we will be limited by our emotional and physical well-being.

However, when *relying on God's strength* to work in and through us, mercy does not come from our own depth of care for others. It flows from a never-ending well of compassion that continues even when we're empty. God whispers words of hope and life to us to express to others, all the while lifting us up as well when we use our gifts. Hospitality is no longer limited by margin, but is creatively expressed through unique opportunities to serve and love others well. When we live out of our gifts, our gifts transform us.

Word of Knowledge, Teaching, Healing. When working in our own strength, we still have advice to give, but it may be limited to our surface understanding of a given situation. Teaching can become more systematic and less inspirational.

The desire to communicate will be fueled by what needs to be learned, rather than by the hearts of those desiring to learn. And we may still pray for healing, but lack the connection to understand how [we are] meant to intercede as one gifted to speak healing over others.

However, when we rely on God's strength to work in and through us, we are given instruction, counsel, and wisdom directly from Him. This usually supersedes anything that can be seen on the surface or inferred from it.

We've cultivated the discipline of listening and waiting on Him to reveal that truth. We teach with supernatural assistance to those who desire to learn and find ourselves overcoming obstacles that limit our own understanding. We're innovative in the way we communicate, and we witness God connecting the dots from information to understanding.

When we rely on God to work through us, we pray for healing and believe that we are God's messenger in that time of need. Although this gift is sometimes misunderstood, we know that ultimate healing will come by the power of Jesus Christ in this life or the next. We can pray, lay hands on, anoint, and speak life into those who need spiritual and/or physical restoration, believing that God is working through us at all times. When we live out of our gifts, our gifts transform us.

As our minds are being renewed, our new way of thinking begins to dictate our behavior. Transformation happens when our understanding of our gifts begins to express itself in reliance on God to live ON purpose FOR purpose. We've been entrusted with awesome abilities; it's our responsibility to risk, leverage, and use those gifts, and they will grow!

However, Jesus gives us a stern warning in the parable of the talents. He not only describes for us the amazing results when we risk, leverage, and use our giftedness, but He also warns us about the consequences of not using them.

> *"To those who use well what they are given, even more will be given, and they will have an abundance. But from those who do nothing, even what little they have will be taken away"* (Matthew 25:29).

When we use our gifts, they grow. They grow in strength and ability as they transform us from the inside out. However, when we settle for false transformation and behavior modification through our own strength, what little was given can and will be taken away.

OUR GIFTS TRANSFORM OTHERS

One of the strongest arguments I can make for the reason God has supernaturally given each Christ follower special gifts and abilities is to help others change as well. The purpose of a gift of leadership, or a gift of discernment, or even the gift of apostleship, is not only to transform us (although it will) but also to help bring others back to God.

> *"This means that anyone who belongs to Christ has become a new person. The old life is gone; a new life has begun! And all of this is a **gift** from God, who brought us back to himself through Christ. And God has given us this task of reconciling people to Him"* (2 Corinthians 5:17–18).

We are not only gifted with our new life by God, but we are also called to use our giftedness to help others reconcile with Him.

As God changes our own hearts and minds, the natural outcome should be a life that points others to Him. As we grow in using our gifts to strengthen the body, we also grow in our desire to reach others for God. This is the result of true transformation. Not that we simply "perfect" the use of a spiritual gift, but that in using our gifts, we point others to the absolute Hope of Jesus Christ.

GIFTS IN REAL LIFE

Prophecy, Giving, Tongues. Paul tells Timothy to preach God's Truth (His Word) to correct, rebuke, and encourage others (2 Timothy 4:2). When using the gift of **prophecy**, you're driven to speak His Word. The prophets of old were given special revelations from God. His Word is now complete (Revelation 22:18–19), and today, prophets carry the urgency to proclaim His Truth to a watching world. When words are not enough, our **generosity** in giving often speaks louder than words. Being generous with all our resources (time, talents, treasures) adds value to others and is another way we declare who God is to a watching world. Paul reminds us that the gift of **tongues** was a sign to unbelievers (1 Corinthians 14:22), so pray that God would use it to reveal His Power and Glory to those who witness it. These miraculous gifts were given to be seen in the context of the body of Christ; let your gift of tongues signify the strength of the body.

I'll never forget my friend telling me of a woman with the gift of prophecy who spoke truth into his life at precisely the moment he needed it most. He was on the verge of making a devastating decision that would have derailed his purpose, and her words—delivered with gentle authority—stopped him in his tracks. She didn't know his entire situation; she simply followed the Spirit's prompting to share what God had placed on her heart. Years later, he credits that moment as the turning point that set him on his current path of ministry. Her gift, used ON purpose FOR purpose, didn't just transform her—it completely redirected my friend's life, who is serving full-time in ministry today!

Shepherd, Apostle, Faith. The Great **Shepherd** cares for his people (Hebrews 13:20), and those with this gift reflect the heart of God to others. What a fantastic way for others to experience God through the gift of someone who deeply cares and walks with them through life. The **apostle's** gift is to leap forward, crush through glass ceilings, and risk much for the kingdom of God. They are entrepreneurs and fire starters in ministry and industry. They display the creativity and innovation of a creative and innovative God to a watching world. **Faith** allows you to crush the spirit of fear in the most challenging circumstances. Faith does not point people to a blind optimism but rather to the clarity of the God in whom they trust with all their heart, mind, and strength.

When the body of Christ is strengthened and individual members are transformed through the use of their gifts, God is glorified for the whole world to witness. When we allow our gifts to transform us, we also use or leverage them to help people reconcile with God.

At Journey Church (where I serve), our vision states that we are "Transformed People Changing Our Friends' Lives By Absolute Hope." We can only accomplish this by relying on the power within to change us first, so we can help change the world ON purpose FOR purpose!

Reflection Questions

1. Reflect on the three C's of false transformation (conforming, comparing, condemning). Which of these has been your default approach when trying to grow spiritually? How has this affected your ability to live fully in your gifts?

2. Think about a time when you operated in your gifting through your own strength versus a time when you relied completely on the Holy Spirit. What differences did you notice in the experience and outcome?

3. The chapter states that "transformation starts in the mind." What specific thought patterns or beliefs do you need to renew in order to more fully embrace and operate in your spiritual gifts?

4. How have you seen your spiritual gifts transform you over time? What areas of your character have been most affected by exercising your gifts on purpose FOR purpose?

5. In what specific way could you use your primary spiritual gift this week to help transform someone else's life or perspective? What step will you take to intentionally do this?

6

GIFTED FOR IMPACT

> *God has given each of you a gift from his great variety of spiritual gifts. Use them well to serve one another.*
>
> —1 Peter 4:10

One of the greatest revelations we receive when we dive into understanding our giftedness is the profound impact our gifts can have on others. Our gifts (just read through the list again) are designed and given to us for the benefit of one another, to strengthen and encourage the body of Christ (the church), and to reveal the power of God to a watching world.

Peter reminds us that each one of us has been gifted, and we must use those gifts well to serve one another.

Have you ever dropped a pebble in a still pond and watched the ripples spread outward? That's what happens when you begin living ON purpose FOR purpose. Your gifts create ripples that extend far beyond your immediate circle, touching the lives of people you may never even meet. Every gift you've been given was strategically placed within you by God to create a specific impact in specific places at specific times. Nothing about your spiritual design is accidental!

According to Matthew, in the days before his crucifixion, Jesus taught a series of parables that led to a powerful illustration of our impact. In the parable of the Three Servants (parable on stewardship), Jesus explained what it will be like when the "King" welcomes those of His servants to His Kingdom. He said:

For I was hungry, and you fed me. I was thirsty, and you gave me a drink. I was a stranger, and you invited me into your home. I was naked, and you gave me clothing. I was sick, and you cared for me. I was in prison, and you visited me. Then these righteous ones will reply, "Lord, when did we ever see you hungry and feed you? Or thirsty and give you something to drink? Or a stranger and show you hospitality? Or naked and give you clothing? When did we ever see you sick or in prison and visit you?" And the King will say, "I tell you the truth, when you did it to one of the least of these my brothers and sisters, you were doing it to me!"

Then the King will turn to those on the left and say, "Away with you, you cursed ones, into the eternal fire prepared for the devil and his demons. For I was hungry, and you didn't feed me. I was thirsty, and you didn't give me a drink. I was a stranger, and you didn't invite me into your home. I was naked, and you didn't give me clothing. I was sick and in prison, and you didn't visit me." Then they will reply, "Lord, when did we ever see you hungry or thirsty or a stranger or naked or sick or in prison, and not help you?" And he will answer, "I tell you the truth, when you refused to help the least of these my brothers and sisters, you were refusing to help me." And they will go away into eternal punishment, but the righteous will go into eternal life (Matthew 25:35–46).

Jesus gave us an everyday example of how having an impact on others will impact us for eternity. For those who use their gifts to meet the needs of those around them, to have an impact on their lives, and to help those who are hurting and in need, you will be welcomed into the Kingdom. However, if you fail to reach those you see every day, those who are hurting and in need because you ignored or simply separated yourself from them, you will be cursed and cast out of the Kingdom.

Based on the entirety of the gospel, Jesus was not suddenly inserting some sort of legalistic maze of "how to get to heaven" for those seeking a key. However, Jesus always made sure that when speaking to "his servants," they understood the powerful impact they *can* have on others and that this matters for eternity. Following the parable of the three servants, Jesus drew a clear connection between those who use and leverage what has been gifted (entrusted) to them and those who bury that gift in the ground.

> *"To those who use well what they are given, even more will be given, and they will have an abundance. But from those who do nothing, even what little they have will be taken away"* (Matthew 25:29).

The greater the calling, the greater the consequence. This is clear when Jesus gives a simple example of serving someone in the most tangible way (to clothe, to feed, to visit, to care for) and attaches the highest reward to it: "The King will welcome you home." We often assume that a great calling is to "end world hunger," which is indeed a very noble work. However, Jesus considered these tangible acts a great calling, saying, "When you do any of this to the least of these my brothers, you did it to me." He wanted us to know that to serve one matters because that one represents Him.

> **TO SERVE ONE MATTERS BECAUSE THAT ONE REPRESENTS HIM.**

I remember meeting an elderly woman at one of my past churches who had the spiritual gift of encouragement. She never stood on a stage or led a ministry, but every Sunday she positioned herself near the entrance to greet people with genuine warmth. Years later, after she passed away, we discovered that dozens of people had been profoundly impacted by her simple greeting. She never knew the impact she had made with her seemingly small gift.

MAKE A DIFFERENCE, NOT A POINT

I'm not sure who originally made this statement (everyone on Google claims it's their own), but I first heard it in a sermon by a pastor from Atlanta named Andy Stanley. Since then, I've used it often to help people understand that making a difference and making a point are two very different things.

Even those who desire to make a difference struggle to *live in their difference* and to understand that each person is unique and uniquely gifted. God isn't calling us to *uniformity*, but rather *unity* through Christ. This unity is not seen when our primary goal is to prove others wrong so we can be right.

For the past 50 years, most Christians have been content with making a point. As keepers of the Truth (the Word of God), it seems as if everyone has simply decided their gift is "prophecy" and has been satisfied to launch "truth grenades" into crowds of unbelievers with the expectation that telling them "we're right" and "you are wrong" is all we are required to do.

We've forgotten our calling in Matthew 25.

Had Jesus said, "Just make sure to tell that naked person they're naked, and you're good. I'll welcome you into the Kingdom," then our assault with truth grenades would be an effective strategy. That would be making a point!

As much as I love the connectivity that social media has brought to our culture today, it has done no favors in helping us actually make a difference in people's lives, but rather fuels our inclination (in 280 characters or in a meme) to simply make a point.

We are gifted for impact.

We are gifted ON purpose FOR purpose.

We are gifted with the ability to make a difference in people's lives. Even the gift of prophecy (sharing God's Word) is given to us to [encourage] and build up the church, not to tear down those who don't claim to believe in God to begin with (1 Corinthians 14).

I believe that most people actually want to make a difference in people's lives, but we've lost sight of how to do it and what it will cost us.

Making a difference does cost us something. It requires us to connect with and serve those we've been called to love, as Christ loved us. This is a required cost of using our gifts for impact. We must first and foremost have love.

A BETTER WAY TO LIVE

For those who dive deep into the context, Paul's letter to the church in Corinth has an interesting structure. The end of his letter is where he addressed the "concerns" the church members had about how and what these spiritual gifts were. Remember, he said, *"I don't want you to misunderstand this"* (1 Corinthians 12:1).

After Paul gave a detailed description of the gifts given to us by the Holy Spirit (manifestation gifts), he gave us the picture of the body of Christ (like a human body) and its many parts. However, the transitional statement that led into the famous "LOVE" chapter (with sections read at most weddings) was this:

> *"You should earnestly desire the most helpful gifts. But now let me show you a way of life that is best of all"* (1 Corinthians 12:31).

What a great setup statement! I could only imagine the folks at the church of Corinth hearing this read aloud for the first time by one of their leaders. Hearing the incredible words of God written to them through Paul, they must have been sitting on the edge of their seats. "A better way to live? I wonder what that is? Tell us, Paul. Tell us!"

Picture yourself sitting among the Corinthians, your mind swirling with questions about these spiritual gifts you've been hearing about. You're possibly even feeling a bit competitive about which gifts are "better." Then Paul drops this bombshell—there's a way of life that transcends all this gift-ranking and comparison. Can you feel the anticipation building? What could possibly be more important than these supernatural abilities?

For the next seven verses, Paul talked about *the impact of LOVE:* that if he could do all kinds of miracles, but didn't have love, it meant nothing. Even if he could understand all the mysteries of God, if he didn't love, then he understood nothing. If he could speak with heavenly tongues of angels, but didn't have love, then it would just be noise! Then came the "love" verses.

> *Love is patient and kind. Love is not jealous or boastful or proud or rude. It does not demand its own way. It is not irritable, and it keeps no record of being wronged. It does not rejoice about injustice but rejoices whenever the truth wins out. Love never gives up, never loses faith, is always hopeful, and endures through every circumstance. Love never fails* (1 Corinthians 13:4–8).

At this point, I think everyone in Corinth must have been silenced by these words. What a powerful description of love that God gave us through Paul's letter. He specifically called out 2 gifts, prophecy and tongues (most scholars assume they were arguing about which one was greater based on the content of 1 Corinthians 14). Paul stressed that the impact of these gifts is temporary, but love lasts forever.

Then Paul, in the most humble way possible, declared how little we actually know about these things. Not that we are completely ignorant; after all, Paul wanted them to better understand these things. However, he stated very clearly that even what little we know is *"seen imperfectly, like puzzling reflections in a mirror"* (1 Corinthians 13:12).

Then he transitioned one more time into the last part of his letter about the use of these gifts with this statement:

> *"Three things will last forever—faith, hope, and love—and the greatest of these is love"* (1 Corinthians 13:13).

> **LOVE IS THE FUEL FOR THE IMPACT WE CAN MAKE WITH OUR GIFTEDNESS.**

Love does not negate our giftedness. Paul's challenge to the church in Corinth was not "forget that gift junk, just LOVE EVERYBODY #lovewins." The reason Chapter 13 is placed right in the middle of his long discussion about the use of spiritual gifts is because love is the FUEL for the IMPACT we can make with our giftedness.

Paul is giving us insight into "how" our gifts make an impact on others; it's through love. Love is the fuel that drives our impact, helping us leverage and use our giftedness in our everyday lives to make a difference in the lives of others we come into contact with.

Just think about how differently we would see our spiritual gifts through the lens of LOVE.

Prophecy—The Truth of God, spoken with love, is not used like ammo in a gun to destroy people. It's the love of God (written in His Word) that draws people to Him. It's His "kindness that leads us to repentance" (Romans 2:4).

Teaching—To communicate God's Truth in such a way that people can connect and understand it. This should not be driven by debates, arguments, and selfish apologetics. If we "love" the people we are teaching, then we will not be satisfied with merely declaring or communicating the truth in the way we prefer, but will be driven to ensure it connects with those we are teaching.

Leadership—To lead others is not simply a position of authority and power. God calls us to lead others in love (John 13:12–17). We're called to motivate, encourage, and hold accountable those we lead, with a heart to see them succeed and do better than they could on their own.

Apostleship—The entrepreneurial spirit deep inside of apostles is necessary in the church today. However, this is not driven by risk and reward (financial) as the world perceives it. The drive of our innovators is their love for the Church—to see it gain influence and break cultural barriers. These objectives propel us to meet needs and serve our communities with hope and love!

Special Knowledge—This miraculous gift can be hard to receive since we have no clear way to judge someone's internal motivation. That is why love matters so much more in gifts that come through miraculous signs. Not only should we receive that special knowledge with a heart of love for God who gave it to us, as well as to the hearer, but to pray over the timing, location, and tone by which we deliver this "Word" to others. *"If we have not love, it is a noisy gong or a clanging cymbal"* (1 Corinthians 13:1).

Distinguishing Between Spirits (Discernment)—This gift is also hard to judge by internal motivation. Discernment isn't given to help us cut through the clutter and noise of words and excuses to identify a root issue or hear what the soul is saying. Love drives us to discern for another's benefit; to understand something more clearly. Love directs better questions and encourages by helping to clarify what is at the heart of their concerns.

Wisdom—As through the example of Solomon, this gift is not driven by a picture of who is right or wrong. The gift of wisdom is primarily found in the choices we make. When love is the driving force behind the gift of wisdom, it's never used to condemn, but to lovingly warn. It's not used to embarrass or mock those who lack wisdom, but to teach and encourage them in love.

I once witnessed the tremendous difference between a gift used with love versus one used without it. Two people in our church had the gift of discernment. One used it like a weapon, always "discerning" others' faults and announcing them publicly—creating fear, not freedom. The other used the same gift with profound love, privately approaching people with compassionate questions rather than accusations. The first person's ministry eventually collapsed under the weight of relational damage. The second person's quiet ministry continues to help people experience breakthrough and healing. Same gift—vastly different impact—because one operated ON purpose FOR purpose through love.

LOVE MULTIPLIES OUR IMPACT

Jesus emphasized love so much, we have to work incredibly hard to miss it.

"Your love for one another will prove to the world that you are my disciples" (John 13:35).

I don't think Jesus was careless with His words. Especially those words that would overwrite 3000 years of Jewish law in one statement. Jesus gave them one command that we, too, should follow, which fulfills all the laws of the prophets in the past: *"to love one another the way that Jesus has loved us."* This is how "the world" will know that we are His disciples.

The World? Really?

The reason Jesus was able to make this statement (outside of being the omniscient God) is because of the Gifted Impact Multiplication Principle^{IP}: love multiplies the impact we are able to make when we live ON purpose FOR purpose. When we are fueled by love, our actions have a resounding impact that goes farther and faster than we could possibly imagine. It reaches those we may never personally meet.

> **LOVE DOESN'T DIMINISH THE EFFECTIVENESS OF YOUR GIFT; IT MULTIPLIES IT EXPONENTIALLY!**

Think about the difference between an arrow and a firework. An arrow can hit one target with precision—that's making a point. But a firework explodes in all directions, illuminating the darkness for everyone within sight—that's love-fueled impact. Your gifts, when powered by love, aren't just precision instruments targeting individuals; they're expansive forces that light up entire communities. Love doesn't diminish the effectiveness of your gift; it multiplies it exponentially!

Love is the ultimate amplifier of our spiritual gifts. It takes what God has already placed within you and maximizes its impact in ways you could never engineer on your own. This is what it means to live ON purpose FOR purpose—using exactly what God has given you, exactly where He's placed you, fueled by the supernatural power of His love.

Are you ready to stop making points and start making a difference? Are you willing to let love be the driving force behind your unique giftedness? The world doesn't need more clever arguments or impressive displays of spiritual power. It needs you—fully alive in your gifts, completely surrendered to love, intentionally creating impact wherever God has placed you.

This is your invitation. This is your purpose. This is your moment to live ON purpose FOR purpose!

Reflection Questions

1. Think about a time when someone used their spiritual gift in a way that profoundly impacted you. What made their impact so significant? How was love evident in how they used their gift?

2. In what situations do you find yourself more focused on "making a point" rather than "making a difference"? What would change if you approached these situations with the primary goal of loving people rather than being right?

3. Which of your spiritual gifts do you need to intentionally reframe through the lens of love? How might this shift in perspective change the way you use this gift and the impact it has?

4. Jesus taught that when we serve "the least of these," we're actually serving Him. Who are "the least of these" in your specific sphere of influence that your gifts are uniquely positioned to impact?

5. What's one concrete step you can take this week to maximize the impact of your primary spiritual gift by intentionally coupling it with love? How will this help you live more fully on purpose FOR purpose?

PART 2

Your Gifts Profile

This part is what I call the Gifts Codex^{IP}. There are three primary categories of gifts (Motivational, Ministry, and Manifestation) given to us by the Father, the Son, and the Holy Spirit. There is one God who is the source of all gifts, and they are only broken up in this manner to reflect the context of how they are given to us in Scripture.

Please take an assessment (revisit Chapter 3) to help you study the Gifts Codex. I will list all resources used to create this glossary in the Resource section of this book, but don't stop there. Read as much as you can on your spiritual gifts. I have no doubt that God will use additional resources to help you grow in your understanding of your gifts and how to use them.

7

MOTIVATIONAL GIFTS

SEVEN GIFTS GIVEN BY GOD THE FATHER

Prophecy, Serving Others (Helps), Teaching, Giving, Encouragement, Leadership, Mercy

> *In His grace, God has given us different gifts for doing certain things well. So if God has given you the ability to prophesy, speak out with as much faith as God has given you. If your gift is serving others, serve them well. If you are a teacher, teach well. If your gift is to encourage others, be encouraging. If it is giving, give generously. If God has given you leadership ability, take the responsibility seriously. And if you have a gift for showing kindness to others, do it gladly.*
>
> —Romans 12:6–8

The gifts given to us by God the Father are most commonly known as the Motivational Gifts. They are also referred to as Enabling Gifts, Administrative Gifts, Redemptive Gifts, or Aptitude Gifts. Listed in Romans 12:6–8, they seem to characterize basic motivations or inherent tendencies in a person that align with God's purpose in their initial gifting. Paul writes it in such a way that it seems to indicate that they might "already be doing these things," so just do them with an understanding that God has given you that gift.

I've listed each gift with additional Scriptural references (context), some characteristics of how they work in your life, and any warnings or additional research that might benefit your understanding of these gifts.

PROPHECY

The divine strength to communicate God's truth in a way that calls people to a right relationship with God.

> NOTE: The "Prophecy" gift is repeated in the Motivational Gifts, Ministry Gifts, and Manifestation Gifts sections. Although there may be a slight variation in the use and function of this gift based on biblical scholars' understanding of the roles associated with it, it retains the same foundational characteristics. For this reason, the following definition and support Scripture are repeated in all three gifts sections.

Scripture Foundation

> "But everyone who prophesies speaks to people for their strengthening, encouraging and comfort" (1 Corinthians 14:3).

Additional References: Acts 2:37–40, 7:51–53, 26:24–29; 1 Thessalonians 1:5

Prophecy is an English word derived from the Greek word *propheteia*, as used by Paul in his letter to the Corinthians. *Propheteia* is translated as either *prophecy* or *prophesying* throughout the New Testament, and *Strong's Exhaustive*

Concordance of the Bible best defines it as "prediction (scriptural or other)."[4]

You Might Have This Gift If...

- You're wired with a strong sense of right and wrong that feels almost like a spiritual compass.
- You see the world in clear moral terms rather than shades of gray.
- You find yourself unable to compromise on deeply-held convictions, even when it would be easier.
- You often feel a holy urgency to challenge destructive patterns in others' lives.
- People describe you as "principled" or say you have "strong convictions."
- You're willing to stand firm for truth even when it makes you unpopular.
- You naturally filter situations through "What does God's Word say about this?"
- You feel a deep responsibility to speak truth, even when others remain silent.

Watch Out For...

- **TRUTH WITHOUT LOVE**—Remember, prophecy without love is just noise (1 Cor. 13:2).
- **JUDGMENT VS. DISCERNMENT**—Be careful not to condemn people while confronting actions.
- **TIMING MATTERS**—Even a perfect truth delivered at the wrong time can be rejected.

- **THE MESSENGER'S HEART**—Check your motives: Are you speaking to build up or to prove you're right?

Strengthen This Gift By...

- **SCRIPTURE IMMERSION**—Your prophetic gift is most powerful when aligned with God's written Word.
- **PRACTICING COMPASSION**—Intentionally see the person behind the behavior you're addressing.
- **SEEKING FEEDBACK**—Ask trusted friends if your delivery matches your heart.
- **PRAYER PARTNERSHIP**—Find prayer partners who will cover you when you exercise this gift.

Biblical Examples

- **NATHAN** confronted King David with "You are the man!" after his sin with Bathsheba.
- **ESTHER** risked everything to speak truth to power: "If I perish, I perish."
- **JOHN THE BAPTIST** fearlessly called people to repentance and preparation.
- **PAUL** addressed the Athenians by connecting to their cultural understanding before delivering truth.

Modern Application

The prophetic voice today speaks God's unchanging truth into our changing world. Whether addressing social justice issues, calling out corruption in systems, or confronting personal sin in love, prophetic people pull back the curtain on what's really happening beneath the surface. Your gift helps others see situations as God sees them.

While the Old Testament prophets often predicted future events, today's prophetic gift primarily forth-tells (speaks God's truth) rather than foretells (predicts future events).

Gift in Action

THE SETTING: Your small group is discussing a popular self-help book that subtly contradicts biblical teaching.

PROPHETIC RESPONSE: While others focus on the helpful elements, you sense something isn't right. Instead of dismissing the entire book or attacking those who like it, you thoughtfully identify specific points that contradict Scripture, helping the group discern truth from error.

You might say: "I appreciate how this book helps people take responsibility for their lives, but I'm concerned about the way it defines success primarily through achievement rather than Christ-likeness. What if we examined these principles through a biblical filter?"

Power Combinations

- **PROPHECY + MERCY** = Truth delivered with remarkable compassion
- **PROPHECY + TEACHING** = Biblical principles explained with conviction and clarity
- **PROPHECY + ENCOURAGEMENT** = Truth that inspires positive action rather than shame

> **Reflection Questions**
>
> 1. When was the last time you felt compelled to speak truth when others remained silent?
> 2. How has God used your straightforward perspective to help others see situations more clearly?
> 3. In what areas might God be calling you to develop more grace in your truth-telling?
> 4. What truth do you sense God asking you to speak right now? To whom? How?

Future-tellers?

Let's add some clarity to what many believe is the gifting (or office) of prophecy. The prophets of the Old Testament had a remarkable gift and duty to speak the Word of God to His people, and to foretell events and outcomes based on what they heard from God. This is similar to how the Gift of prophecy works today, except that we (followers of Christ) now have God's Word given to us through the Holy Spirit's inspiration of the written Scriptures.

"The work of the Old-Testament prophets was not only to foretell future things, but to warn the people concerning sin and duty, and to be their remembrancers concerning that which they knew before. And thus gospel preachers are prophets, and do indeed, as far as the revelation of the word goes, foretell things to come."[5]

"Those with the gift of prophecy speak the truth of God's Word under the guidance of the Holy Spirit."[6]

This is not to say that those with a specific mixture of gifts (discernment, special knowledge) won't combine them with their gift of prophecy to proclaim Truth with a supernatural understanding of something that we could not ordinarily know (special knowledge) or see in our present state (discernment). When we consider these gift mixes, we understand how one might confuse the gift of prophecy with the Old Testament calling (and office) of a Prophet. While the powerful gift of prophecy remains, the office of a future-telling intermediary on God's behalf does not.

- When exercising your gift of prophecy, speak it boldly with Scriptural wisdom. All prophecy from God will align with God's written Word. Allow space for the Holy Spirit to confirm the word of prophecy you share with someone in their hearts. Be cautious of assigning or insinuating a timeline of your prophecy unless it's supported within the written Word of God.
- When receiving a word of prophecy from someone, use Scriptural wisdom in receiving it. Does it align with the Truth of God's Word? Be cautious of what is claimed as a "new revelation." Has the Holy Spirit within given you peace and confirmation? Is there a timeline insinuated, and if so, are you able to discern if that timing is from God or from the giver of that prophecy?

SERVING (HELPS)

The divine strength to do practical tasks, large or small, that meet needs and support others in their ministry.

Scripture Foundation

"For even the Son of Man did not come to be served, but to serve, and to give his life as a ransom for many." (Mark 10:45)

Additional References: Acts 6:1–7; Romans 12:7; Galatians 6:10; 1 Timothy 1:16–18; Titus 3:14

You Might Have This Gift If…

- You find deep satisfaction in completing practical tasks that help others succeed.
- You're often the first to notice when something needs to be done and the first to do it.
- You prefer working behind the scenes rather than in the spotlight.
- You're motivated by responsibility and completion, not recognition.
- You create to-do lists for the pure joy of checking things off.
- You notice details others miss.
- You work effectively without supervision or constant encouragement.
- You feel frustrated when others talk about needs but don't take action.

Watch Out For…

- **BURNOUT**—Your willingness to serve can lead to overcommitment.

- **RESENTMENT**—Serving without healthy boundaries can breed bitterness.
- **ENABLING**—Sometimes helping actually prevents others from growing.
- **IDENTITY IN DOING**—Remember your worth isn't tied to how much you accomplish.

Strengthen This Gift By...

- **PARTNERING UP**—Find ministry teams where your behind-the-scenes work multiplies impact.
- **SETTING BOUNDARIES**—Learn to say "yes" to your best contribution, not every request.
- **SPIRITUAL REFRESHMENT**—Schedule regular time to be served by God through worship and rest.
- **SKILL DEVELOPMENT**—Identify and hone specific skills that make your service more effective.

Biblical Examples

- **MARTHA** served Jesus and his disciples with practical hospitality.
- **TABITHA (DORCAS)** made clothing for widows and the poor in her community.
- **ONESIPHORUS** refreshed Paul and wasn't ashamed of his chains.
- **PHOEBE** was commended as a faithful servant of the church in Cenchreae.

Modern Application

In our self-focused culture, servants stand out like stars in the night sky. Your gift creates atmospheres where ministry happens smoothly. Whether setting up chairs, preparing meals, handling administrative tasks, or maintaining facilities, your behind-the-scenes work often determines whether a ministry succeeds or fails. Far from being "just helping," your gift reflects Christ's heart: "I am among you as one who serves" (Luke 22:27).

Gift in Action

THE SETTING: Your church is planning a community outreach event, but the leadership team is overwhelmed by the logistics.

SERVING RESPONSE: While others debate program details, you quietly create a comprehensive checklist of needed supplies, potential volunteers, and timeline benchmarks. You handle the practical details that would distract others from their primary roles.

You might say: "I've prepared this event checklist—would it help if I coordinated the setup team so you can focus on connecting with our guests?"

Power Combinations

- **SERVING + LEADERSHIP** = Servant leadership that inspires others through example
- **SERVING + ENCOURAGEMENT** = Practical help delivered with uplifting words
- **SERVING + GIVING** = Generosity expressed through both resources and actions

> ### *Reflection Questions*
>
> 1. What behind-the-scenes tasks bring you the greatest sense of fulfillment?
> 2. How has God used your practical service to open doors for ministry that might otherwise remain closed?
> 3. Are there areas where your serving has become duty rather than delight? How might you refresh your perspective?
> 4. What need do you see that others are overlooking right now? How might God be calling you to address it?

The Overlooked Thankless Gifting

Here's what breaks my heart about the serving gift: You've probably never been properly thanked. Not really. See, when you stayed late to stack chairs, you were worshiping. When you cleaned up after the event everyone else celebrated at, you were walking in the footsteps of Jesus, who washed feet. You have spiritual X-ray vision for incompleteness—that crooked picture frame, the overflowing trash can during the prayer meeting, the single mom who needs her oil changed but will never ask. You can't unsee it. Most people don't even know these needs exist until you've already met them.

But here's the holy truth: every table you set becomes an altar. **Every behind-the-scenes task preaches a sermon about the Kingdom where the last are first.** In a world that worships platforms and spotlights, your gift feels invisible. Instagram doesn't capture the beauty of cleaned bathrooms or organized supply closets. But Heaven sees. Heaven celebrates. You're not "just helping"—you're embodying the mystery of a God who chose to reveal His glory through a servant's towel.

So here's your permission slip: You don't have to do it all. Really. The building won't collapse if you take a Sabbath. Jesus served perfectly and completely—you're just called to serve faithfully and wisely. **Your worth isn't in your usefulness** but in who you are. When you serve the least of these with excellence and love, you're holding up a mirror to the face of God. That's not helping out. That's holy ground.

TEACHING

> *NOTE: The "Teaching" gift is repeated in the Motivational Gifts and Ministry Gifts sections. Although there may be slight variations in the use and function of this gift depending on some scholars' understanding of the roles associated with it, it retains the same foundational characteristics. For this reason, the following definition and support Scripture are repeated in both gifts sections.*

The divine strength to understand and communicate biblical truth in clear, transformative ways.

> The Greek word for those with the spiritual gift of teaching is *didaskalos*. The root of this gives us the English word "didactic." The word *didasko* means to teach, instill doctrine, instruct, and explain.[7]

Scripture Foundation

"Let the message of Christ dwell among you richly as you teach and admonish one another with all wisdom." (Colossians 3:16)

Additional References: Acts 18:24–28, 20:20–21; 1 Corinthians 12:28; Ephesians 4:11–14

You Might Have This Gift If...

- You have a knack for making complex ideas understandable.
- You're driven to explain not just what to do but how and why.
- People often say you helped them "connect the dots" spiritually.
- You naturally gather examples, illustrations, and applications to support the truth.
- You're energized by watching others grasp a concept for the first time.
- You're bothered by incomplete or inaccurate information.
- You enjoy researching and delving deeper into topics.
- You find yourself thinking about the best way to explain something.

Watch Out For...

- **INFORMATION OVERLOAD**—More content doesn't always mean more impact.

- **INTELLECT WITHOUT APPLICATION**—Knowledge without transformation misses the point.
- **PRIDE IN KNOWLEDGE**—Remember, "knowledge puffs up while love builds up" (1 Cor. 8:1).
- **NEGLECTING RELATIONSHIPS**—Truth is best received in the context of trust.

Strengthen This Gift By...

- **BECOMING A LEARNER**—The best teachers never stop being students.
- **DIVERSIFYING METHODS**—Develop multiple ways to communicate for different learning styles.
- **SEEKING FEEDBACK**—Ask listeners what connected and what confused.
- **LIVING THE TRUTH**—Embody the principles you teach; authenticity multiplies impact.

Biblical Examples

- **EZRA** devoted himself to studying, observing, and teaching God's Word.
- **PRISCILLA AND AQUILA** explained the way of God more adequately to Apollos.
- **APOLLOS** refuted the Jews in public debate, showing from Scripture that Jesus was the Messiah.
- **JESUS** taught with stories, questions, object lessons, and life examples.

Modern Application

In an age of information overload, teachers with spiritual depth are desperately needed. Your gift helps believers move beyond spiritual milk to solid food, equipping them to discern truth from error. Whether teaching Sunday school, leading Bible studies, mentoring individuals, or creating resources, you build the foundation that supports every other ministry. As Jesus demonstrated, effective teaching isn't just transferring information—it's transformation through illumination.

Gift in Action

THE SETTING: A new believer asks you a difficult theological question that has them confused and doubting.

TEACHING RESPONSE: Rather than giving a simplistic answer, you break the concept down into understandable pieces, using analogies from their everyday lives. You patiently address their specific confusion points and provide Scripture references they can explore further.

You might say: "That's a great question! Think about it this way..." (followed by a clear illustration). "Does that help make sense of it? Let's look at a few passages together that address this..."

Power Combinations

- **TEACHING + PROPHECY** = Truth explained with compelling conviction
- **TEACHING + ENCOURAGEMENT** = Instruction that inspires and motivates

- **TEACHING + MERCY** = Patient explanation tailored to individual needs

> ### Reflection Questions
>
> 1. What biblical topics or passages do you find yourself naturally drawn to study deeply?
> 2. When have you experienced the joy of seeing someone grasp a spiritual truth through your explanation?
> 3. How might God be calling you to develop your teaching skills beyond your current comfort zone?
> 4. Who has been a model teacher in your life? What qualities made their teaching effective?

Teacher Plus (Additional Gifts)

Teachers have been entrusted with the task of effectively communicating what the Bible says, what it means, and how we as followers of Jesus Christ are to apply it to our lives here and now. James 3:1 warns, "*...not many of you should become teachers in the church, for we who teach will be judged more strictly.*" As believers, we are to be stewards of every word that comes out of our mouths, but even greater responsibility falls on those who teach to be careful stewards of the Word of God to His people.

The best part of the teaching gift is that it looks different with every personality and gift mix. A mix of a teaching gift and a prophetic gift might come across as stoic and callous, while a mix of a teaching gift and an encouraging gift might look like a motivational speaker. The important thing to remember about the teaching gifts is that, regardless of how it comes out, you are instrumental in helping people learn, grow, and apply Biblical truths to their lives.

Luke's work in writing Scriptural accounts was driven by a desire to verify and preserve the truth about both Jesus' life and the formation of the Church so that the faith of believers would be strengthened. Luke tells us, *"Having carefully investigated everything from the beginning, I also have decided to write an accurate account for you, most honorable Theophilus, so you can be certain of the truth of everything you were taught"* (Luke 1:3–4). It's clear that Luke used his additional gifts to strengthen his teaching gift when recording an accurate account for us.

GIVING

The divine strength to contribute resources generously, cheerfully, and strategically for Kingdom impact.

Scripture Foundation

> *"Remember this: Whoever sows sparingly will also reap sparingly, and whoever sows generously will also reap generously. Each of you should give what you have decided in your heart to give, not reluctantly or under compulsion, for God loves a cheerful giver"* (2 Corinthians 9:6–7).

Additional References: Mark 12:41–44; Romans 12:8; 2 Corinthians 8:1–7, 9:2–7

You Might Have This Gift If...

- You find deep joy in providing resources that meet needs and advance ministry.
- You're good at managing finances and often generate surplus resources.
- You don't need recognition for your giving but love seeing the impact it makes.
- You think strategically about how to maximize the effectiveness of every dollar.
- You're sensitive to genuine needs that others might overlook.
- You see money as a tool for Kingdom work, not as a means of personal security.
- You give spontaneously and often anonymously.
- You feel a supernatural nudge to give at specific moments.

Watch Out For...

- **ENABLING DEPENDENCY**—Sometimes, financial help without accountability creates harm.
- **SUBSTITUTING MONEY FOR TIME**—Remember that presence can be more valuable than presents.
- **PRIDE IN PROVISION**—Guard against a subtle sense of superiority in being the provider.
- **UNBALANCED GIVING**—Even givers need financial wisdom and boundaries.

Strengthen This Gift By...

- **DEVELOPING FINANCIAL WISDOM**—Learn stewardship principles that multiply your impact.
- **BUILDING RELATIONSHIPS**—Connect with ministries to understand their needs beyond money.
- **PRAYER-GUIDED GIVING**—Ask God for divine appointments with needs you're uniquely positioned to meet.
- **CREATING GIVING STRATEGIES**—Plan your giving thoughtfully while remaining open to Spirit-led spontaneity.

Biblical Examples

- **THE WIDOW** gave her last two coins, demonstrating sacrificial generosity.
- **BARNABAS** sold a field and laid the money at the apostles' feet.
- **MACEDONIAN CHURCHES** gave beyond their ability, despite extreme poverty.
- **LYDIA** supported Paul's missionary work with her business resources.

Modern Application

In a materialistic culture, Kingdom givers demonstrate a radical alternative to accumulation and self-focus. Your gift extends ministry far beyond what would otherwise be possible. Whether funding missions, supporting church plants, meeting emergency needs, or providing for the overlooked, your generosity creates ripples of impact that continue long after the initial gift is made. You are a living demonstration that God's economy operates on principles different from those of the world.

Gift in Action

THE SETTING: Your church announces a mission trip that will impact an unreached people group, but several key youth can't afford to participate.

GIVING RESPONSE: Without fanfare, you provide scholarships for these students through the youth pastor, requesting that the funding source remain anonymous. You recognize that this isn't just about money, but about an eternal impact.

You might pray: "Lord, thank you for entrusting me with resources that can open doors for your Gospel. Use these funds not just to send these young people, but to transform both them and those they'll reach."

Power Combinations

- **GIVING + DISCERNMENT** = Resources directed with supernatural insight to strategic needs
- **GIVING + ENCOURAGEMENT** = Financial support accompanied by words that build faith
- **GIVING + LEADERSHIP** = Vision-casting backed by resources to make it happen

> ### Reflection Questions
>
> 1. How has God developed your understanding of stewardship over time?
> 2. What was your most joyful giving experience? What made it especially meaningful?
> 3. Are there ways God might be calling you to give beyond financial resources (time, skills, possessions)?
> 4. How might you cultivate even greater sensitivity to the Holy Spirit's guidance in your giving?

Aren't We ALL Called to Give?

Yes, we all have a responsibility to give back (tithes and offerings) and be generous with what God has given us (Matthew 25). However, the gift of giving has often been attributed to those whom God has given a great capacity to create wealth. The primary purpose of creating wealth (for a person with this gift) is to be able to give generously (above and beyond). Generosity is the call of all believers, but God has given some a special gift and divine capacity to do more.

ENCOURAGEMENT (EXHORTATION)

The divine strength to motivate, strengthen, and urge others forward in their faith journey.

Scripture Foundation

"But encourage one another daily, as long as it is called 'Today,' so that none of you may be hardened by sin's deceitfulness" (Hebrews 3:13).

Additional References: Acts 14:22; Romans 12:8; 1 Timothy 4:13; Hebrews 10:24–25

You Might Have This Gift If...

- You naturally notice potential in others that they often don't see in themselves.
- You're drawn to people who are struggling, discouraged, or at turning points.
- You're an attentive listener who asks insightful questions.
- You instinctively find the positive angle in challenging situations.
- You communicate hope even as you acknowledge difficult realities.
- You're passionate about helping others take their next spiritual step.
- You hate working alone and thrive on relational connections.
- You celebrate others' successes as enthusiastically as your own.

Watch Out For...

- **AVOIDING HARD TRUTH**—Sometimes encouragement requires loving confrontation.
- **OVERWHELMING OTHERS**—Your enthusiasm might sometimes feel pressuring.
- **SUPERFICIAL CHEERLEADING**—Genuine encouragement goes deeper than positive platitudes.
- **NEGLECTING SELF-CARE**—You can't effectively encourage others from an empty well.

Strengthen This Gift By...

- **SCRIPTURE MEMORIZATION**—Store up biblical promises and truths to share at the right moment.
- **ACTIVE LISTENING**—Develop the discipline of fully focusing on others without formulating responses.
- **ASKING POWERFUL QUESTIONS**—Learn to ask questions that help others discover truth for themselves.
- **FOLLOW-UP SYSTEMS**—Create ways to consistently check in with those you've encouraged.

Biblical Examples

- **BARNABAS** ("Son of Encouragement") advocated for Paul when others were suspicious.
- **PAUL** wrote letters strengthening new believers and young churches.

- **JONATHAN** encouraged David in the wilderness when he was fleeing from Saul.
- **RUTH** pledged her loyalty to Naomi when returning would have been easier.

Modern Application

In our culture of criticism and comparison, encouragers are spiritual oases in the desert. Your gift creates safe spaces where others find strength to continue their journey. Whether mentoring individuals, leading support groups, writing notes of affirmation, or simply being present in difficult seasons, you embody the ministry of presence. Your words and actions literally "put courage into" others when they need it most.

Gift in Action

THE SETTING: A friend confides that they're considering abandoning a God-given dream because of repeated setbacks and criticism.

ENCOURAGEMENT RESPONSE: You listen deeply, validate their struggle, then reflect back the evidence of God's calling you've observed in their life. You share a relevant scriptural example of perseverance, then suggest a specific next step they can take.

You might say: "I hear your discouragement, and those obstacles are real. But I've watched God consistently open doors despite the challenges. Remember Joseph's story? His dream took 13 years and a prison cell to fulfill. What's one small step you could take this week to keep moving forward?"

Power Combinations

- **ENCOURAGEMENT + WISDOM** = Motivation paired with sound guidance
- **ENCOURAGEMENT + FAITH** = Inspiration that builds supernatural confidence
- **ENCOURAGEMENT + DISCERNMENT** = Affirmation that addresses the real underlying issue

---

Reflection Questions

1. Who has been your most significant encourager? What specific things did they do or say that strengthened you?
2. When have you seen your words or presence make a turning-point difference for someone?
3. What group of people do you feel especially drawn to encourage (e.g., leaders, new believers, the grieving)?
4. How might God be calling you to develop greater depth or specificity in your encouragement?

Unlock The Power Within

Paul addressed the questions and concerns of the early believers and challenged them to be faithful in their walk with God. *"... this is the secret: Christ lives in you. This gives you assurance of sharing his glory. So we tell others about Christ, warning everyone and teaching everyone with all the wisdom God has given us. We want to present them to God, perfect in their relationship to Christ.*

That's why I work and struggle so hard, depending on Christ's mighty power that works within me" (Colossians 1:27–29 NIV).

LEADERSHIP

> NOTE: This gift often overlaps with other gifts listed on assessments, such as Administration or Organization.

The divine strength to cast vision, motivate, and guide people toward God's purposes.

Scripture Foundation

"Be shepherds of God's flock that is under your care, watching over them—not because you must, but because you are willing, as God wants you to be; not pursuing dishonest gain, but eager to serve; not lording it over those entrusted to you, but being examples to the flock" (1 Peter 5:2–3).

Additional References: Romans 12:8; 1 Timothy 3:1–13, 5:17; Hebrews 13:17

You Might Have This Gift If...

- You naturally see the big picture when others get caught in the details.
- You enjoy mobilizing people around a compelling vision or goal.
- You intuitively create systems that help people work together effectively.

- You're energized by developing other leaders, not just followers.
- You take initiative in ambiguous situations where direction is needed.
- You're willing to make difficult decisions that others might avoid.
- You see potential problems and opportunities before they become obvious.
- You naturally influence others even without formal authority.

Watch Out For...

- **TASK OVER PEOPLE**—Remember that people aren't projects or tools to accomplish goals.
- **CONTROL ISSUES**—True biblical leadership empowers others rather than micromanaging.
- **IMPATIENCE**—Not everyone processes or moves at the same pace you do.
- **LONE RANGER SYNDROME**—Even strong leaders need accountability and support.

Strengthen This Gift By...

- **DEVELOPING SELF-AWARENESS**—Understand your leadership style, strengths, and blind spots.
- **BUILDING A STRONG TEAM**—Surround yourself with people whose gifts complement yours.
- **CULTIVATING HUMILITY**—Study Jesus' servant leadership model.

- **SEEKING MENTORSHIP**—Find experienced leaders who will speak truth into your life.

Biblical Examples

- **NEHEMIAH** cast vision, organized workers, and overcame opposition to rebuild Jerusalem's walls.
- **DEBORAH** provided clear direction and courage when others hesitated.
- **PETER** stepped forward at Pentecost to guide the early church through its formative days.
- **PAUL** established and oversaw multiple churches, developing leaders in each location.

Modern Application

In an era of leadership crisis, Spirit-empowered leaders stand out by serving rather than being served. Your gift helps turn divine possibility into earthly reality. Whether leading a small group, ministry team, organization, or movement, you help others see where God is leading and how to get there together. Unlike worldly leadership that "lords it over" others, your leadership follows Jesus' model: "Whoever wants to become great among you must be your servant" (Mark 10:43).

Gift in Action

THE SETTING: Your church has identified a community need, but efforts to address it have been scattered and ineffective.

LEADERSHIP RESPONSE: You gather key stakeholders, help clarify the vision, identify obstacles, and develop a strategic plan with clear next steps. Most importantly, you identify and empower the right people to execute each part of the plan.

You might say: "I believe God is calling us to meet this need, but we'll be more effective working together strategically. Here's what success might look like... What gifts do we have among us that God has already provided for this work? Who should take point on each aspect?"

Power Combinations

- **LEADERSHIP + SERVING** = Servant leadership that inspires through example
- **LEADERSHIP + WISDOM** = Strategic direction informed by godly insight
- **LEADERSHIP + ENCOURAGEMENT** = Vision-casting that motivates and energizes

Reflection Questions

1. What type of leadership contexts energize you most? What settings drain you?
2. Who has modeled Christ-like leadership in your life? What specific qualities made their leadership effective?
3. How has God been developing your leadership character through challenges or failures?
4. What current situation might God be calling you to step forward and lead, even without a formal invitation?

Servant Leadership

One of the ways you can spot a leadership gift from God is in the way they serve others, not by exercising power over them. "Wait, Matt. I thought serving was a helpful gift, right?" Yes, that is serving; however, leading others through serving is the example we are given through the life and leadership of Jesus Christ.

In Matthew 20:25, Jesus painted the picture of leadership that is of this world: leadership where those in power and authority "*lord it over their people, and officials flaunt their authority over those under them.*" But Jesus said, "*not so with you...*" His powerful words described a new type of leadership, evidenced by one who comes to serve. For whoever wants to be a leader must become a servant. This is the primary distinction between someone with a leadership gift versus someone who simply has positional authority or temporary power.

MERCY

The divine strength to feel deeply for those who are hurting and respond with practical compassion.

Scripture Foundation

> "*Blessed are the merciful, for they will be shown mercy*" (Matthew 5:7).

Additional References: Matthew 9:35–36; Mark 9:41; Romans 12:8; 1 Thessalonians 5:14

You Might Have This Gift If...

- You're deeply moved by others' pain and suffering, even strangers'.
- You instinctively see beyond behavior to the hurt that drives it.
- You're willing to enter messy situations others avoid.
- You're more inclined to show compassion first, then address issues later.
- You become uncomfortable when others are harshly judged or criticized.
- You easily empathize with people whose struggles you haven't personally experienced.
- You're drawn to the most broken or overlooked people in any group.
- You sometimes physically feel others' emotional pain.

Watch Out For...

- **EMOTIONAL DRAINAGE**—Compassion fatigue is real and requires intentional self-care.
- **ENABLING UNHEALTHY PATTERNS**—Sometimes, mercy without accountability perpetuates problems.
- **AVOIDING NECESSARY CONFRONTATION**—Love sometimes requires difficult conversations.
- **ABSORBING OTHERS' EMOTIONS**—Learn to empathize without taking on others' emotional burdens.

Strengthen This Gift By...

- **ESTABLISHING BOUNDARIES**—Even Jesus didn't heal everyone; learn to discern where to focus.
- **PARTNERING WITH OTHERS**—Team up with those whose gifts complement mercy with truth and wisdom.
- **DEVELOPING RESILIENCE**—Build practices that replenish your emotional reserves.
- **PRAYER COVERING**—Surround your mercy ministry with consistent prayer support.

Biblical Examples

- **THE GOOD SAMARITAN** crossed cultural barriers to help a wounded stranger.
- **JESUS** was moved with compassion for the sick, grieving, and outcast.
- **TABITHA (DORCAS)** made clothes for widows and showed practical kindness.
- **THE PHILIPPIAN JAILER** washed Paul and Silas's wounds after their beating.

Modern Application

In our hurried, often indifferent world, mercy-givers reflect the heart of Jesus, who was "moved with compassion" when he saw suffering. Your gift creates safe spaces for those who are wounded to heal. Whether visiting the homebound, supporting those in crisis, working with the marginalized, or simply being present with the grieving, you embody God's tender care for those who are broken. You remind us that Christianity is not just about believing right but loving well.

Gift in Action

THE SETTING: A family in your church is overwhelmed by a serious diagnosis that has created practical, emotional, and spiritual challenges.

MERCY RESPONSE: While others offer advice or spiritual platitudes, you show up consistently with practical help, a listening ear, and comfortable silence when needed. You intuitively understand what will truly help rather than burden them further.

You might say: "I'm dropping off dinner Tuesday. I've arranged for someone to mow your lawn weekly, and I'll sit with John during treatment on Thursday so you can get a break. No need to entertain me or even talk—I'm just here to walk alongside you however you need."

Power Combinations

- **MERCY + PROPHECY** = Compassion that speaks truth with perfect timing
- **MERCY + WISDOM** = Heart-led care guided by divine insight
- **MERCY + SERVING** = Practical compassion that meets tangible needs

> **Reflection Questions**
>
> 1. When have you felt God's pleasure as you extended mercy to someone in need?
> 2. What specific populations or types of suffering especially break your heart?
> 3. How do you maintain healthy boundaries while still showing genuine compassion?
> 4. What current situation is God inviting you to enter with His heart of mercy?

The Cost of Mercy

Here's the thing about mercy that nobody tells you up front: It will cost you everything and give you everything all at once. See, the world has a version of compassion that looks good on social media—a quick donation, a sad emoji, maybe a prayer comment. But the mercy gift? That's something else entirely.

When God gives you this gift, He's inviting you into His own heartbreak. Remember when Jesus looked at the crowds and was "moved with compassion" because they were like sheep without a shepherd? That Greek word literally means His guts were wrenched. This is visceral stuff. You don't just see pain—you *feel* it in places you didn't know existed.

And here's the beautiful challenge: mercy without boundaries becomes enabling, but boundaries without mercy become walls. You're called to live in that messy middle space where love stays soft but wisdom stays sharp. Where you can weep with those who weep without drowning in their tears. Where you enter the darkness with others but refuse to let it become your home.

Listen, if you have this gift, you already know the exhaustion of caring too much. You've probably been called "too sensitive" or "bleeding heart." Good. The world desperately needs hearts that still bleed in an age of increasing indifference. But—and this is crucial—Jesus modeled something radical: He regularly withdrew to lonely places to pray. Even the Savior of the world knew that pouring out required filling up.

So lean in. Feel deeply. Show up in the mess. But remember: You're not the Messiah. You're simply called to reflect His mercy, one broken person to another. That's enough. That's everything.

8

MINISTRY GIFTS

FIVE GIFTS GIVEN BY JESUS CHRIST

Apostle, Prophet, Evangelist, Shepherd (Pastor), Teacher

> *Now these are the gifts Christ gave to the church: the **apostles**, the **prophets**, the **evangelists**, and the **pastors and teachers**. Their responsibility is to equip God's people to do his work and build up the church, the body of Christ.*
>
> —Ephesians 4:11–12

The gifts given to us by Jesus Christ are most commonly known as the Ministry Gifts. They are also referred to as Office Gifts, Equipping Gifts, and Team Gifts. Listed in Ephesians 4:11–12, they are stated with a specific purpose. Jesus gave these gifts to the "church." This refers to "ecclesia" (a movement, gathering) and is not referring to the organizational church but rather to the entire body of Christ (people) that comprises the Kingdom of God. They are also described with further purpose in verse 12 that they are to be used "to equip God's people (the Church) to do His work, and build up the Church—the body of Christ."

APOSTLE

The divine strength to pioneer new works, establish foundations, and empower emerging leaders with entrepreneurial vision.

Scripture Foundation

> *"For I am the least of the apostles and do not even deserve to be called an apostle, because I persecuted the church of God. But by the grace of God I am what I am, and his grace to me was not without effect"* (1 Corinthians 15:9–10).

Additional References: Acts 15:22–35; 1 Corinthians 12:28; 2 Corinthians 12:12; Galatians 2:7–10; Ephesians 4:11–14

You Might Have This Gift If...

- You're energized by starting new initiatives, ministries, or communities.
- You thrive on challenges others consider impossible or impractical.
- You see potential and possibility where others see only problems.
- You naturally develop systems that can be replicated and multiplied.
- You're willing to take significant risks for kingdom advancement.
- You have a unique ability to identify and develop emerging leaders.

- You think in terms of multiplication rather than addition.
- You're restless when things become too comfortable or predictable.
- You navigate change and uncertainty with unusual confidence.

Watch Out For...

- **RELATIONAL WAKE**—Moving too quickly can leave people feeling used or abandoned.
- **UNFINISHED BUSINESS**—Not everything God calls you to start, He calls you to finish.
- **AUTHORITY ISSUES**—Remember that pioneering doesn't exempt you from accountability.
- **INNOVATION IDOL**—Sometimes, steadfastness is more needed than the next new thing.

Strengthen This Gift By...

- **STRATEGIC PARTNERSHIPS**—Find faithful implementers who can steward what you start.
- **ACCOUNTABILITY STRUCTURES**—Establish safeguards that keep your pioneering spirit healthy.
- **CROSS-CULTURAL EXPOSURE**—Your gift thrives when challenged by diverse perspectives.
- **LONG-TERM VISION**—Develop the discipline of seeing beyond the exciting launch phase.

Biblical Examples

- **PAUL** established churches throughout the Roman world, never building on another's foundation.
- **BARNABAS** identified emerging leaders like Paul and John Mark when others missed their potential.
- **PETER** crossed cultural barriers to bring the gospel to Gentiles against all conventions.
- **PRISCILLA AND AQUILA** established ministry training centers wherever they went.

Modern Application

In our rapidly changing world, apostolic leaders aren't just church-planters—they're kingdom-minded entrepreneurs who see opportunity where others see chaos. Your gift helps the church break free from "we've always done it this way" thinking. Whether establishing new ministries, creating innovative outreach strategies, pioneering in unreached areas, or building reproducing discipleship systems, you're wired to push beyond comfortable boundaries. You remind the church that its edges should expand, not contract.

Gift in Action

THE SETTING: Your church has been struggling to reach the growing immigrant population in your community, as traditional outreach methods have proven ineffective.

APOSTOLIC RESPONSE: Rather than tweaking existing programs, you envision an entirely new approach. You identify and empower leaders from within the immigrant community, establish a self-reproducing discipleship model, and create pathways for new believers to immediately begin sharing their faith within their networks.

You might say: "What if instead of inviting them to come to us, we equipped them to reach their own people? Let's identify potential leaders within that community, provide targeted training, and create a model that can multiply without our constant oversight."

Power Combinations

- **APOSTLE + SHEPHERD** = Pioneering leadership that doesn't sacrifice relational depth
- **APOSTLE + TEACHING** = Innovative approaches that remain doctrinally sound
- **APOSTLE + EVANGELIST** = Multiplication strategies with soul-winning effectiveness

Reflection Questions

1. What existing structures or methods might God be calling you to respectfully challenge?
2. Where do you see unreached people or unmet needs that require fresh approaches?
3. Who are the emerging leaders God has placed in your path to identify and develop?
4. What current "impossibility" is stirring your apostolic vision and imagination?

Like the Apostle Paul?

The *spiritual gift* of apostleship is sometimes confused with the *office* of Apostle. The office of Apostle was held by a limited number of men chosen by Jesus, including the twelve disciples (Mark 3:13–19) and Paul (Romans 1:1). The Apostles were given authority by Jesus to establish the Church, teach (and write) about Jesus, and perform miracles (John 14:26, 2 Peter 3:15–16, 2 Corinthians 12:12).

Those with the gift of apostleship today are challenged to lead new ministries and churches. They develop leaders and equip pastors and shepherds who lead leaders. They also lead the charge to go where the Gospel is not yet preached, are typically entrepreneurial leaders of leaders, able to take risks, and perform difficult tasks with deep conviction. They are the spiritual and cultural influencers of the organized church.

PROPHET

> *NOTE: The "Prophecy" gift is repeated in the Motivational Gifts, Ministry Gifts, and Manifestation Gifts sections. Although there may be slight variations in the use and function of this gift based on biblical scholars' understanding of the roles associated with it, it retains the same foundational characteristics. For this reason, the following definition and support Scripture are repeated in all three gifts sections.*

The divine strength to discern God's truth and proclaim it with clarity, conviction, and authority.

Scripture Foundation

"But the one who prophesies speaks to people for their strengthening, encouragement and comfort" (1 Corinthians 14:3).

Additional References: Acts 2:37–40, 7:51–53, 26:24–29; 1 Corinthians 14:1–4; 1 Thessalonians 1:5

Prophecy is an English word derived from the Greek word *propheteia,* as used by Paul in his letter to the Corinthians. *Propheteia* is translated as either *prophecy* or *prophesying* throughout the New Testament, and Strong's Concordance best defines it as "prediction (scriptural or other)."[8]

You Might Have This Gift If...

- You carry a profound sense of God's holiness and humanity's accountability.
- You can identify foundational issues when others are distracted by symptoms.
- You have a deep conviction about the alignment between belief and practice.
- You're able to see through cultural facades to underlying spiritual realities.
- You experience unusual boldness when speaking God's truth.
- You're deeply troubled by hypocrisy, especially in the church.
- You have a heightened sensitivity to God's voice and direction.
- You feel a sense of urgency about calling God's people back to authentic faith.

Watch Out For...

- **HARSH DELIVERY**—Remember that prophetic truth is for building up, not tearing down.
- **BLACK-AND-WHITE THINKING**—Complex situations sometimes require a nuanced understanding.
- **ISOLATION**—Prophetic perspectives can lead to loneliness without intentional community.
- **PRIDE IN PERCEPTION**—Seeing what others miss is a gift to steward, not a weapon to wield.

Strengthen This Gift By...

- **DEEP SCRIPTURE ENGAGEMENT**—Your prophetic gift is authenticated by alignment with God's Word.
- **PRAYER IMMERSION**—Cultivate intimate dialogue with God to ensure you're speaking His heart.
- **MENTORSHIP**—Find seasoned prophetic voices who will help you mature in your gift.
- **COMMUNITY GROUNDING**—Submit your insights to wise counsel and the body of Christ.

Biblical Examples

- **ISAIAH** called a nation to repentance through powerful imagery and convicting messages.
- **NATHAN** confronted King David with laser-focused truth at a pivotal moment.

- **DEBORAH** provided clear divine guidance in a time of national confusion.
- **AGABUS** accurately predicted coming events to help the church prepare.

Modern Application

In an age of compromise and confusion, prophetic voices call the church back to its authentic identity and mission. Your gift helps God's people distinguish between cultural Christianity and the reality of the Kingdom. Whether addressing systemic injustice, exposing theological drift, calling out misaligned priorities, or revealing God's activity in current events, you function as a spiritual compass. You remind us that God's perspective on our world often differs radically from conventional wisdom or popular opinion.

Gift in Action

THE SETTING: Your church has been gradually accommodating cultural values that subtly contradict biblical teaching, with most members unaware of the drift.

PROPHETIC RESPONSE: Rather than attacking individuals, you prayerfully identify the specific areas of compromise and their root causes. You present this insight with both boldness and love, calling for a return to foundational truths while offering a path forward.

You might say: "I believe God is showing me that we've slowly exchanged biblical faithfulness for cultural acceptance in these specific areas. The good news is that God is extending grace to us, allowing us to realign with His heart. What if we committed to examining every aspect of our community through the lens of Scripture rather than current trends?"

Power Combinations

- **PROPHET + MERCY** = Truth delivered with remarkable compassion and kindness
- **PROPHET + SHEPHERD** = Correction that heals rather than wounds
- **PROPHET + WISDOM** = Insights paired with practical application steps

Reflection Questions

1. What specific messages or insights do you sense God consistently bringing to your attention?
2. How have you experienced both the cost and calling of speaking unpopular truth?
3. In what ways does your prophetic perspective need tempering with other perspectives?
4. What specific area of compromise or drift might God be calling you to lovingly address?

Future-tellers?

Let's add some clarity to what many believe is the gifting (or office) of prophecy. The prophets of the Old Testament had a remarkable gift and duty to speak the Word of God to His people, and to foretell events and outcomes based on what they heard from God. This is similar to how the Gift of prophecy works today, except that we (followers of Christ) now have God's Word given to us through the Holy Spirit's inspiration of the written Scriptures.

"The work of the Old-Testament prophets was not only to foretell future things, but to warn the people concerning sin and duty, and to be their remembrancers concerning that which they knew before. And thus gospel preachers are prophets, and do indeed, as far as the revelation of the word goes, foretell things to come."[9]

"Those with the gift of prophecy speak the truth of God's Word under the guidance of the Holy Spirit."[10]

This is not to say that those with a specific mixture of gifts (discernment, special knowledge) won't combine them with their gift of prophecy to proclaim Truth with a supernatural understanding of something that we could not ordinarily know (special knowledge) or see in our present state (discernment). When we consider these gift mixes, we understand how one might confuse the gift of prophecy with the Old Testament calling (and office) of a Prophet. While the powerful gift of prophecy remains, the office of a future-telling intermediary on God's behalf does not.

- When exercising your gift of prophecy, speak it boldly with Scriptural wisdom. All prophecy from God will align with God's written Word. Allow space for the Holy Spirit to confirm the word of prophecy you share with someone in their hearts. Be cautious of assigning or insinuating a timeline of your prophecy unless it's supported within the written Word of God.
- When receiving a word of prophecy from someone, use Scriptural wisdom in receiving it. Does it align with the Truth of God's Word? Be cautious of what is claimed as a "new revelation." Has the Holy Spirit within given you peace and confirmation? Is there a

timeline insinuated, and if so, are you able to discern if that timing is from God or from the giver of that prophecy?

EVANGELIST

The divine strength to share the good news of Jesus with exceptional clarity and effectiveness.

> The Greek word for evangelist is euaggelistes, which means "one who brings good news." This word occurs only twice in the New Testament: Acts 21:8 and 2 Timothy 4:5.

Scripture Foundation

"But you, keep your head in all situations, endure hardship, do the work of an evangelist, discharge all the duties of your ministry" (2 Timothy 4:5).

Additional References: Acts 8:5–6, 8:26–40, 14:21, 21:8; Ephesians 4:11–14

You Might Have This Gift If...

- You naturally turn conversations toward spiritual matters.
- You genuinely feel excited when sharing your faith.
- You see redemptive potential in people others might write off.

- You experience unusual boldness when explaining the gospel.
- You're deeply burdened for those who don't know Jesus.
- You regularly think about how to make faith accessible to non-believers.
- You celebrate enthusiastically when someone makes a faith commitment.
- You're constantly noticing opportunities to share God's love.
- You find it relatively easy to build rapport with people far from faith.

Watch Out For...

- **SUCCESS METRICS**—Remember that faithfulness, not numbers, is your responsibility.
- **SHALLOW CONVERSIONS**—Focus on making disciples, not just decisions.
- **EVANGELISTIC SUPERIORITY**—Every believer is called to witness; your gift equips but doesn't exempt others.
- **RELATIONAL SHORTCUTS**—People aren't projects; authentic relationships matter.

Strengthen This Gift By...

- **CULTURAL FLUENCY**—Learn to translate timeless truth into relevant language for different audiences.

- **STORY PREPARATION**—Develop clear, compelling ways to share both your testimony and the gospel.
- **PARTNERSHIP DEVELOPMENT**—Connect with those gifted in discipleship to ensure new believers grow.
- **CONTINUOUS LEARNING**—Study how the gospel addresses today's questions and objections.

Biblical Examples

- **PHILIP** followed divine guidance to share Christ with an Ethiopian official at the perfect moment.
- **THE SAMARITAN WOMAN** immediately told her village about Jesus after her encounter with Him.
- **PAUL** contextualized the gospel differently for Jewish and Greek audiences.
- **PETER** boldly proclaimed Christ at Pentecost, leading thousands to faith.

Modern Application

In our post-Christian culture, evangelists are more crucial than ever—not as bullhorn-wielding street preachers, but as clear translators of God's love and truth. Your gift helps bridge the growing gap between church language and everyday life. Whether engaging skeptics, equipping believers to share their faith, creating environments where seekers feel welcome, or simply modeling authentic Christian witness, you demonstrate that evangelism isn't a program but a lifestyle of invitation. You remind the church that its message remains "good news" in a world desperate for hope.

Gift in Action

THE SETTING: Your workplace includes several colleagues who express curiosity about faith but feel alienated by religious institutions and language.

EVANGELISTIC RESPONSE: Rather than inviting them to church events, you create natural opportunities for spiritual conversation. You host dinner gatherings where life's big questions can be discussed openly, share your faith journey in relevant bits as opportunities arise, and look for practical ways to demonstrate Christ's love.

You might say: "I'm hosting a dinner next Friday for friends to discuss life's big questions—no agenda, just authentic conversation. Several of us have different perspectives on faith, and I'd love to include your voice if you're interested."

Power Combinations

- **EVANGELIST + MERCY** = Soul-winning combined with practical compassion
- **EVANGELIST + WISDOM** = Gospel clarity that addresses life's deepest questions
- **EVANGELIST + TEACHER** = Faith sharing that builds strong foundations

Reflection Questions

1. What aspects of the gospel message especially come alive when you share your faith?
2. Which people groups or demographics do you find yourself particularly drawn to reach?

> 3. How has God uniquely shaped your story to help specific types of people connect with Him?
> 4. What barriers might be preventing you from fully exercising your evangelistic gift?

Isn't This Everyone's Job?

In short, yes! However, this gift is given to the church because there are those whom God clearly calls to be evangelists. The Apostle Paul was one of them. All Christians were given the charge to share their faith and help lead others to a saving relationship with Jesus Christ—but clearly, Paul had a "gift" for it! Driven by a passion and zeal to make sure EVERYONE heard the gospel, Paul traveled farther around the known world than all the other apostles combined!

Evangelists, by the Holy Spirit, can clearly communicate the Gospel of Jesus to others. Their heart breaks for those who do not know Jesus as their personal Savior. Evangelists can overcome fear and obstacles that would hinder most folks from engaging those who are far from God. They love deep conversations about faith and the Hope that is found in Jesus. In their giftedness, they can reach across racial and socioeconomic divides to share the Good News. They work hard to build relationships with "outsiders" and non-believers to lead them to God.

SHEPHERD (PASTOR)

The divine strength to nurture, protect, and guide people toward spiritual maturity.

> The Greek word for pastor is *poimen* and simply means shepherd or overseer.

Scripture Foundation

> *"Be shepherds of God's flock that is under your care, watching over them—not because you must, but because you are willing, as God wants you to be"* (1 Peter 5:2).

Additional References: John 10:1–18; Ephesians 4:11–14; 1 Timothy 3:1–7; 1 Peter 5:1–3

You Might Have This Gift If...

- You're deeply fulfilled when helping others grow spiritually.
- You intuitively notice when someone is hurting or struggling.
- You naturally build trust that invites people to be authentic with you.
- You feel a protective concern for others' well-being.
- You're willing to walk with people through messy, long-term challenges.
- You find joy in celebrating others' spiritual victories, however small.
- You're drawn to restoring the broken and strengthening the weak.
- You think about people's needs and spiritual development throughout your week.

- You create environments where people feel safe, seen, and supported.

Watch Out For...

- **COMPASSION FATIGUE**—Even the Good Shepherd regularly withdrew to be with the Father.
- **RESCUING VS. EMPOWERING**—Sometimes the most loving response is allowing people to experience the consequences of their actions.
- **CONFLICT AVOIDANCE**—True shepherding sometimes requires difficult conversations.
- **NEGLECTING YOUR OWN SOUL**—You cannot give what you do not possess.

Strengthen This Gift By...

- **HEALTHY BOUNDARIES**—Learn to distinguish between urgent and important needs.
- **SPIRITUAL FORMATION**—Deepen your own walk so you can offer more to others.
- **LEADERSHIP DEVELOPMENT**—Multiply your impact by developing other shepherds.
- **CRISIS PREPARATION**—Equip yourself to guide people through life's darkest valleys.

Biblical Examples

- **DAVID** protected his flock with both tenderness toward the sheep and fierceness toward predators.

- **JESUS** demonstrated the ultimate shepherding model through both individual care and public teaching.
- **BARNABAS** advocated for Mark when others wanted to abandon him after his failure.
- **PAUL** maintained pastoral care for churches even from prison through letters and prayers.

Modern Application

In our increasingly disconnected and isolated culture, genuine shepherds provide essential community and care. Your gift creates spaces where authentic growth can happen. Whether leading a small group, mentoring individuals, providing spiritual direction, or serving in formal pastoral roles, you make the abstract concept of God's care tangible and personal. You model Jesus' words: "I know my sheep and my sheep know me" (John 10:14), reminding us that Christianity thrives in relational soil rather than just institutional structures.

Gift in Action

THE SETTING: A family in your church is experiencing a painful crisis that has spiritual, emotional, and practical dimensions.

SHEPHERDING RESPONSE: Rather than offering quick advice or spiritual platitudes, you come alongside them for the journey. You provide practical support, create a safe space for questions and doubts, offer a biblical perspective when appropriate, and remain steadfast even when progress is slow.

You might say: "I don't have easy answers, but I want you to know you're not walking this road alone. I'm here to listen, to pray with you, to bring meals when needed, and to remind you of God's faithfulness when it's hard to see. We'll take this one day at a time together."

Power Combinations

- **SHEPHERD + WISDOM** = Nurturing care guided by divine insight
- **SHEPHERD + DISCERNMENT** = Spiritual guidance that addresses root issues
- **SHEPHERD + TEACHING** = Pastoral care that builds strong foundations

> ### Reflection Questions
>
> 1. Who has shepherded you well in your spiritual journey? What qualities made their care so impactful?
> 2. What specific aspect of Jesus' shepherding ministry especially resonates with your heart?
> 3. Which types of people or situations naturally awaken your shepherding instincts?
> 4. How is God calling you to grow in both tenderness and courage as a shepherd?

A Shepherd Loves His Sheep

Pastors primarily care for others (like shepherds care for their sheep). They care for the souls entrusted to them by God; this could be an entire church congregation, a small group, or simply a neighborhood. They are first and foremost servants. They serve God, the church, and those in need. They often have a gift mix that allows them to serve needs in their community and overcome obstacles to relate with others.

The Holy Spirit gives the spiritual gift of pastor to some in the church to humbly teach, guide, protect, and lead them in the mission that God has for His church.

TEACHER

> *NOTE: The "Teaching" gift is repeated in the Motivational Gifts and Ministry Gifts sections. Although there may be slight variations in the use and function of this gift depending on some scholars' understanding of the roles associated with it, it retains the same foundational characteristics. For this reason, the following definition and support Scripture are repeated in both gifts sections.*

The divine strength to understand, explain, and apply God's truth with clarity and transformative power.

> The Greek word for those with the spiritual gift of teaching is *didaskalos*. The root of this gives us the English word "didactic." The word *didasko* means to teach, instill doctrine, instruct, and explain.[11]

Scripture Foundation

> *"Not many of you should become teachers, my fellow believers, because you know that we who teach will be judged more strictly"* (James 3:1).

Additional References: Acts 18:24–28, 20:20–21; 1 Corinthians 12:28; Ephesians 4:11–14

You Might Have This Gift If...

- You experience deep satisfaction when someone grasps a spiritual truth.
- You're driven to study Scripture deeply, not just superficially.
- You naturally organize information into understandable patterns.
- You're bothered by incomplete or inaccurate biblical teaching.
- You can make complex theological concepts accessible without watering them down.
- You find yourself mentally creating illustrations to explain biblical principles.
- You're energized by questions that help you clarify your understanding.
- You enjoy the process of researching and preparing to teach.
- You naturally connect biblical truth to practical life application.

Watch Out For...

- **KNOWLEDGE WITHOUT TRANSFORMATION**—The goal is changed lives, not just informed minds.

- **INTELLECTUAL PRIDE**—Remember that "knowledge puffs up while love builds up" (1 Cor. 8:1).
- **OVERWHELMING DETAIL**—Not every teaching opportunity requires exhaustive explanation.
- **RIGIDITY IN APPROACH**—Different people learn through different methods and styles.

Strengthen This Gift By...

- **CONTINUOUS LEARNING**—The best teachers remain perpetual students.
- **METHODOLOGY EXPANSION**—Develop various teaching approaches for different audiences.
- **FEEDBACK CULTIVATION**—Regularly seek input on both content and delivery effectiveness.
- **PRACTICAL APPLICATION**—Always bridge from biblical truth to life implementation.

Biblical Examples

- **EZRA** devoted himself to studying, practicing, and teaching God's law.
- **APOLLO** accurately taught about Jesus but remained teachable when correction was needed.
- **PRISCILLA AND AQUILA** explained the way of God more adequately to Apollo.
- **JESUS** masterfully used questions, stories, and object lessons to make truth unforgettable.

Modern Application

In our information-saturated but wisdom-starved culture, skilled biblical teachers are more essential than ever. Your gift helps believers develop spiritual discernment and depth. Whether teaching classes, writing resources, creating discipleship pathways, or equipping believers one-on-one, you build the foundation upon which other ministries stand. As Paul reminded Timothy, "All Scripture is God-breathed" (2 Tim. 3:16), and your teaching breathes life into ancient texts, helping others see their relevance for today's challenges.

Gift in Action

THE SETTING: Several new believers in your church are struggling to understand fundamental doctrines, leaving them vulnerable to confusion and error.

TEACHING RESPONSE: Rather than overwhelming them with theological jargon, you create a series of accessible sessions that build progressive understanding. You use memorable illustrations, provide practical application points, and create a safe space for questions.

You might say: "Think of the Trinity like water—the same essence can exist as solid ice, liquid water, or vapor steam. The analogy isn't perfect, but it helps us begin grasping how God can be Three-in-One. What questions does that illustration raise for you?"

Power Combinations

- **TEACHER + SHEPHERD** = Instruction delivered with nurturing care

- **TEACHER + PROPHET** = Biblical truth applied with compelling relevance
- **TEACHER + EVANGELIST** = Gospel clarity that draws seekers to understanding

---

Reflection Questions

1. What biblical topics or themes especially energize your teaching passion?
2. Who has modeled effective teaching in your life? What specific qualities made their teaching impact you?
3. How might God be calling you to expand your teaching approach to reach different types of learners?
4. What current confusion or error in the church might God be equipping you to address?

Teacher Plus (Additional Gifts)

Teachers have been entrusted with the task of effectively communicating what the Bible says, what it means, and how we as followers of Jesus Christ are to apply it to our lives here and now. James 3:1 warns, "...not many of you should become teachers in the church, for we who teach will be judged more strictly." As believers, we are to be stewards of every word that comes out of our mouths, but even greater responsibility falls on those who teach to be careful stewards of the Word of God to His people.

The best part of the teaching gift is that it looks different with every personality and gift mix. A teaching gift and a prophetic gift mix might come across as stoic and callous, while a teaching gift and an encouraging gift mix might look like a motivational speaker. The important thing to remember about the teaching gifts is that no matter how it comes out, you are instrumental in helping people learn, grow, and apply Biblical truths to their lives.

Luke's work in writing Scriptural accounts was driven by a desire to verify and preserve the truth about both Jesus' life and the formation of the Church so that the faith of believers would be strengthened. Luke tells us, "Having carefully investigated everything from the beginning, I also have decided to write an accurate account for you, most honorable Theophilus, so you can be certain of the truth of everything you were taught." (Luke 1:3–4). It's clear that Luke used his additional gifts to strengthen his teaching gift when recording an accurate account for us.

A FINAL WORD ON MINISTRY GIFTS

These five gifts weren't randomly distributed. Jesus strategically placed them throughout His body to ensure the church would continue His mission until His return. Some believers express these gifts professionally, but most exercise them without titles or positions.

The question isn't whether you have a ministry gift—it's which one(s) the risen Christ has activated in you for this season. When you discover and deploy your ministry gift(s), you experience deeper fulfillment, the church functions more effectively, and the world witnesses Jesus still at work through His people.

Remember: You were gifted ON purpose FOR purpose. These aren't just abilities—they're divine assignments wrapped in supernatural enablement. Don't compare your gift to others or downplay its significance. Step fully into what Jesus has entrusted to you, and watch what He accomplishes through your yielded life!

9

MANIFESTATION GIFTS

NINE GIFTS GIVEN BY THE HOLY SPIRIT

Wisdom, Special Knowledge, Faith, Healing, Miracles, Prophecy, Distinguishing Between Spirits (Discernment), Tongues, Interpretation of Tongues.

> *To one person the Spirit gives the ability to give wisdom; to another the same Spirit gives a message of special knowledge. The same Spirit gives great faith to another, and to someone else the one Spirit gives the gift of healing. He gives one person the power to perform miracles, and another the ability to prophesy. He gives someone else the ability to discern whether a message is from the Spirit of God or from another spirit. Still another person is given the ability to speak in unknown languages, while another is given the ability to interpret what is being said.*
>
> —1 Corinthians 12:8–10

The gifts given to us by the Holy Spirit are most commonly known as the Manifestation Gifts. They are also referred to as Miraculous Gifts, Edifying Gifts, and Operational Gifts. Listed in 1 Corinthians 12:8–10, these gifts seem to reveal the supernatural power of God in our lives. Although all gifts are supernaturally given, as stated in John 3:6, *"The Holy Spirit gives birth to spiritual life,"* these nine gifts reveal the supernatural power of God within us. Their stated purpose is given in verse 7: "these gifts are given to each of us so we can help each other," indicating that the primary use of these gifts is to benefit the local church body. Paul gave the instruction in verse 31 that *"we should earnestly desire the most helpful gifts."* Paul also addressed specific gifts in 1 Corinthians 14, describing some as external gifts (to reveal God to unbelievers) and others as internal (to bring a message to believers).

> *The Spirit was manifested by the exercise of these gifts; his influence and interest appeared in them. But they were not distributed for the mere honor and advantage of those who had them, but for the benefit of the church, to edify the body, and spread and advance the gospel. Spiritual gifts are bestowed, that men may with them profit the church and promote Christianity. They are not given for show, but for service; not for pomp and ostentation, but for edification; not to magnify those that have them, but to edify others.*[12]

WISDOM

The divine ability to receive and communicate supernatural insight that applies God's truth to specific situations.

Scripture Foundation

> *"For to one is given the word of wisdom through the Spirit, to another the word of knowledge through the same Spirit"* (1 Corinthians 12:8 NKJV).

GIFTED

Additional References: Acts 6:3,10; 1 Corinthians 2:6–13, 12:8; James 1:5–8

You Might Have This Gift If...

- You frequently receive sudden, profound insights that solve complex problems.
- People seek your guidance in difficult or confusing situations.
- You often know exactly what to say in high-pressure moments.
- You can see the underlying principles beneath surface-level issues.
- You recognize patterns and connections that others miss.
- You're able to cut through confusion and identify the heart of a matter.
- You instinctively know how to apply biblical principles to specific circumstances.
- You receive "divine downloads" of understanding that didn't come through natural reasoning.
- You find yourself saying things in counsel that surprise even you with their depth.

Watch Out For...

- **PRIDE IN PERCEPTION**—Remember that this wisdom is a gift, not a personal achievement.
- **SPEAKING PREMATURELY**—Not every insight is meant to be shared immediately or publicly.

- **NEGLECTING SCRIPTURE**—True supernatural wisdom never contradicts God's written Word.
- **BEING MISUNDERSTOOD**—Supernatural wisdom often defies conventional thinking.

Strengthen This Gift By...

- **SCRIPTURE IMMERSION**—Fill your mind with God's Word so your gift flows from His truth.
- **LISTENING PRAYER**—Develop the habit of quieting your thoughts to hear God's voice.
- **FAITHFUL STEWARDSHIP**—Use the gift consistently in small matters to build capacity for larger ones.
- **COMMUNITY DISCERNMENT**—Test your insights within a trusted spiritual community.

Biblical Examples

- **SOLOMON** received divine wisdom to resolve an impossible dispute between two mothers.
- **JOSEPH** interpreted Pharaoh's dreams with supernatural insight, which saved nations.
- **DANIEL** received wisdom beyond human capability to interpret visions and dreams.
- **JESUS** consistently demonstrated perfect wisdom in responding to traps and questions.

Modern Application

In our complex and confusing world, supernatural wisdom cuts through the noise with laser precision. Your gift provides divine guidance when human understanding falls short. Whether resolving conflicts, counseling in crisis, navigating ethical dilemmas, or making pivotal decisions, you receive heaven's perspective on earthly problems. This isn't merely good advice or accumulated experience—it's divine insight for specific situations that leaves people saying, "Only God could have provided that answer."

Gift in Action

THE SETTING: Your church leadership team is deadlocked over a controversial decision with valid concerns on both sides, and relationships are becoming strained.

WISDOM RESPONSE: After prayer, you receive unexpected clarity that reframes the entire situation. Rather than merely compromising, you articulate a third approach that honors the core values of both perspectives while addressing blind spots neither side recognized.

You might say: "I believe God is showing me that we've been looking at this from a perspective of scarcity rather than abundance. What if instead of choosing between these two directions, we..." (sharing the specific insight God has given that transforms the conversation).

Power Combinations

- **WISDOM + DISCERNMENT** = Supernatural insight paired with the ability to detect underlying spiritual dynamics
- **WISDOM + PROPHECY** = Divine guidance delivered with compelling authority
- **WISDOM + TEACHING** = Profound truth communicated with exceptional clarity

---

Reflection Questions

1. When have you experienced a moment of clarity that you knew came directly from God rather than your own understanding?
2. How does God typically deliver supernatural wisdom to you—through thoughts, impressions, dreams, pictures, or other means?
3. What patterns have you noticed regarding when and how this gift activates in your life?
4. What current situation in your life or ministry might need supernatural wisdom rather than just human reasoning?

Quick to Listen, Slow to Respond

One identifier of someone with a gift of wisdom is their willingness to listen and learn more than speak or give counsel. They are hungry in their pursuit of wisdom in any situation, and like James said (James 1:19), they are quick to listen (learn) and pray for wisdom. Many with this gift don't actually feel all that wise, because they are continually learning and don't want to give "bad advice" or something other than wisdom when they speak.

"It's reason, then speech. Intelligence with practical action in accord with it. Speech full of God's wisdom under the impulse of the Spirit."[13]

John Rea, author of *The Layman's Commentary on the Holy Spirit*, offers these insights:

> *[Word of wisdom, word of knowledge, and discerning of spirits] are given to Christians to enable them to know what to do or say in specific situations. Jesus manifested a word of wisdom when, to the Pharisees who were intent on trapping Him with their question about paying a tax to Caesar, He gave His famous reply: "Render to Caesar the things that are Caesar's; and to God the things that are God's" (Matt. 22:21 NASB). He promised us similar wisdom for times of emergency, 'for the Holy Spirit will teach you in that very hour what you ought to say" (Luke 12:12: NASB).*[14]

SPECIAL KNOWLEDGE

The divine ability to receive specific information from God that couldn't be known through natural means.

> The two Greek words used here are *logos* (translated as 'word') and *gnosis* (translated as 'knowledge').
>
> Biblical scholars offer a fairly broad description of this gift, including "a declaration of gospel truth or the application of it," but many scholars agree that a word of knowledge should properly be regarded as a *"supernatural revelation of facts past, present, or future which were not learned through the efforts of the natural mind."* [15]

Scripture Foundation

"To one there is given through the Spirit a message of wisdom, to another a message of knowledge by means of the same Spirit" (1 Corinthians 12:8).

Additional References: Acts 5:1–11; 1 Corinthians 12:8; Colossians 2:2–3

You Might Have This Gift If...

- You receive specific information about people or situations that you couldn't have known naturally.
- You've experienced knowing details about someone's life or needs upon first meeting them.
- You occasionally "just know" things without a logical explanation.
- God reveals specific information to you that helps you minister to others effectively.
- You've accurately perceived physical ailments or emotional wounds in others.
- You sometimes know exactly what Scripture passage someone needs.
- You receive precise insights about situations that help guide prayer or ministry.
- You experience divine "nudges" to contact someone, only to discover they were in crisis.
- You occasionally know the root cause of a problem when only symptoms are visible.

Watch Out For...

- **ATTENTION-SEEKING**—Remember that this gift is to serve others, not to impress them.
- **INAPPROPRIATE DISCLOSURE**—Not all revealed knowledge should be shared publicly.
- **PRESUMPTION**—Distinguish between divine revelation and human assumption.
- **INTRUSION**—Respect boundaries when God reveals sensitive information.

Strengthen This Gift By...

- **DEVELOPING DISCERNMENT**—Learn to distinguish between your thoughts and God's revelation.
- **PRACTICING HUMILITY**—Share what God reveals with gentleness and appropriate timing.
- **PRAYER CULTIVATION**—Deepen your prayer life to enhance your receptivity to God's voice.
- **ACCOUNTABILITY RELATIONSHIPS**—Submit your "words of knowledge" to mature spiritual oversight.

Biblical Examples

- **PETER** supernaturally knew about Ananias and Sapphira's deceit.
- **JESUS** knew the Samaritan woman's marital history without being told.

- **ANANIAS** received specific knowledge about Saul's location and situation.
- **AGABUS** accurately foretold a coming famine through the Spirit.

Modern Application

In our skeptical, information-driven world, supernatural knowledge demonstrates God's intimate awareness of details and needs. Your gift offers divine insight where human knowledge fails. Whether revealing hidden hurts during prayer ministry, identifying specific physical ailments for healing prayer, uncovering root issues in counseling, or receiving strategic information for kingdom advancement, you're given supernatural access to information for the purpose of building up the body of Christ and drawing people to Jesus.

Gift in Action

THE SETTING: During a church prayer gathering, you notice a visitor who seems reserved and disconnected from the group.

KNOWLEDGE RESPONSE: As you pray, you receive a clear impression about a specific childhood trauma they've never disclosed that's creating a barrier in their relationship with God. With appropriate sensitivity, you ask if you can share something God may be showing you about their life.

You might say: "I believe God is showing me that something happened to you around age twelve that's made it difficult to trust Him as a Father. Would it be alright if I pray with you about that specific hurt?"

Power Combinations

- **KNOWLEDGE + HEALING** = Precise insight directing effective healing prayer
- **KNOWLEDGE + MERCY** = Divine insight delivered with profound compassion
- **KNOWLEDGE + WISDOM** = Supernatural information paired with understanding of how to apply it

---

Reflection Questions

1. When have you experienced knowing something you couldn't have known naturally, and how did you respond?
2. How does God typically communicate special knowledge to you—through thoughts, pictures, physical sensations, or other means?
3. What patterns have you noticed regarding when and how this gift activates in your life?
4. How might God want to refine your stewardship of this gift to make it more effective and honoring?

God-Given Knowledge

The spiritual gift of divine knowledge is given when information is needed and when the only way to get that information is through supernatural means: a revelation of God. This goes beyond discernment or clever deduction. In Acts 5:1–11, Peter was given special knowledge to confront the hypocrisy of Ananias and Sapphira concerning the sale of their land and their financial gift to the local church. This special knowledge came from God to help Peter confront their specific sin.

FAITH

The divine ability to believe God for extraordinary interventions with exceptional confidence beyond normal faith.

> In 1 Corinthians 12, the Greek word *pistis* is translated as faith and is defined in Strong's Concordance as "persuasion, i.e., credence; moral conviction (of religious truth or the truthfulness of God or a religious teacher), especially reliance upon Christ for salvation. In the New Testament, pistis is also translated as assurance, belief, believe, and fidelity."[16]

Scripture Foundation

> *"To another faith by the same Spirit, to another gifts of healing by that one Spirit"* (1 Corinthians 12:9).

Additional References: Acts 11:22–24; Romans 4:18–21; 1 Corinthians 12:9; Hebrews 11

You Might Have This Gift If...

- You maintain unwavering confidence in God's promises when others lose hope.
- You see possibilities where others see only obstacles.

- You believe in specific miraculous outcomes with unusual certainty.
- You're drawn to impossible situations that require divine intervention.
- You inspire faith in others during times of crisis or uncertainty.
- You experience supernatural peace about God's provision in dire circumstances.
- You've witnessed God's extraordinary interventions in response to your specific prayers.
- You instinctively claim God's promises over situations without doubting.
- You're energized rather than intimidated by circumstances that have no human solution.

Watch Out For...

- **FAITH WITHOUT WISDOM**—Even supernatural faith should operate with godly wisdom.
- **JUDGING OTHERS' FAITH**—Remember that your gift is not the standard for others.
- **IGNORING PRACTICAL STEPS**—Biblical faith often includes responsible human action.
- **PRESUMPTION**—Distinguish between faith in God's character and assumptions about His specific will.

Strengthen This Gift By...

- **SCRIPTURE SATURATION**—Feed your faith with God's promises and testimonies.

- **FAITH COMMUNITY**—Connect with others who will stand with you in believing in God.
- **TESTIMONIAL JOURNAL**—Record God's faithfulness to fuel future faith challenges.
- **FAITH STRETCHING**—Step into increasingly challenging situations that require supernatural intervention.

Biblical Examples

- **ABRAHAM** believed God's impossible promise despite all natural evidence to the contrary.
- **CALEB** maintained faith for his inheritance through 45 years of wilderness wandering.
- **THE CENTURION** demonstrated such complete faith that Jesus marveled at it.
- **PAUL** maintained absolute confidence in God's deliverance through shipwreck and imprisonment.

Modern Application

In our calculated, risk-averse culture, supernatural faith challenges both church and world to remember that we serve a God of the impossible. Your gift infuses courage when circumstances appear hopeless. Whether believing in miraculous provision, standing firm in spiritual warfare, maintaining vision through prolonged challenges, or claiming God's promises over seemingly impossible situations, you demonstrate that faith is "confidence in what we hope for and assurance about what we do not see" (Hebrews 11:1). Your tenacious belief often becomes the catalyst God uses to display His power.

Gift in Action

THE SETTING: Your church faces an opportunity that requires resources far beyond what seems humanly possible, prompting many to advocate scaling back the vision.

FAITH RESPONSE: While acknowledging the legitimate challenges, you carry an unshakable conviction that God has ordained this vision and will supernaturally provide. You stand firmly on specific promises God has given you, inspiring others to move forward despite the apparent impossibility.

You might say: "I understand the concerns, but I have absolute certainty that God has called us to this. He's shown me that He's already prepared the provision we can't yet see. This isn't wishful thinking—I know it as surely as I know my own name. What specific step of obedience might He be asking us to take first?"

Power Combinations

- **FAITH + WISDOM** = Supernatural confidence guided by divine insight
- **FAITH + LEADERSHIP** = Vision-carrying that inspires others through impossible terrain
- **FAITH + GIVING** = Supernatural provision flowing through extraordinary generosity

> **Reflection Questions**
>
> 1. When have you experienced a level of faith that surprised even you with its unshakable certainty?
> 2. What impossible situation is God currently calling you to believe Him for?
> 3. How does God typically build your faith—through His Word, circumstances, other believers, or other means?
> 4. What external evidence have you seen that confirms your gift of supernatural faith?

Don't We All Have Faith?

> *The spiritual gift of faith is not saving faith (given to believers) but a wonder-working faith like that in Matt 17:20, 21:21.*
>
> —A. T. Robertson, *Word Pictures of the New Testament*

When this gift of faith is in operation, believers have an unshakable confidence that God will do what He has promised to do, even when it seems impossible. (Matthew 17:20, 21:21; Mark 11:22–24; I Corinthians 13:2) As witnessed in Acts 10:20, Peter is prompted to go with the men to Cornelius' house, and Jesus specifically tells him to *"have faith and do not hesitate."*

The spiritual gift of faith is *"a sudden surge of faith, usually in a crisis, to confidently believe without a doubt, that as we act or speak in Jesus' Name it shall come to pass."*[17]

HEALING

The divine strength or ability to act as an intermediary in faith, prayer, and by the laying on of hands for the healing of physical, mental, and spiritual sickness.

> *Strong's Exhaustive Concordance of the Bible* defines *iama* as "a cure (the effect)," and this Greek word is translated only as healing when it is used in the New Testament.[18]

Scripture Foundation

> *"To another gifts of healing by that one Spirit"* (1 Corinthians 12:9).

Additional References: Acts 3:1–10, 9:32–35, 28:7–10; 1 Corinthians 12:9, 28; James 5:14–15

You Might Have This Gift If...

- You're drawn to pray specifically for physical, emotional, or spiritual healing.
- You've witnessed supernatural healing occur through your prayers multiple times.
- You experience unusual compassion toward the sick or injured.
- You sense a specific direction from God about how to pray for someone's healing.
- You often feel prompted to pray for healing even when not requested.

- You maintain strong faith for healing, even when results aren't immediately visible.
- You understand healing as encompassing body, mind, and spirit.
- You experience physical sensations (heat, tingling, etc.) when praying for healing.
- You have a deep conviction that God still heals today as He did in Scripture.

Watch Out For...

- **PERSONAL GLORY**—Remember that Jesus is the healer; you're merely the vessel.
- **FORMULA FIXATION**—Divine healing flows from relationship, not techniques.
- **DISCOURAGEMENT FROM DELAY**—Not all healing manifests immediately or in expected ways.
- **NEGLECTING MEDICAL CARE**—God often works through both supernatural and natural means.

Strengthen This Gift By...

- **HEALING SCRIPTURES**—Immerse yourself in biblical accounts and promises of healing.
- **STEP-BY-STEP OBEDIENCE**—Follow the Spirit's specific guidance for each situation.
- **COMMUNITY OF PRACTICE**—Learn from others with mature healing ministries.
- **GROWING IN AUTHORITY**—Develop confidence in exercising the delegated power of Christ.

Biblical Examples

- **PETER AND JOHN** commanded the lame man to walk at the Beautiful Gate.
- **PAUL** laid hands on Publius' father and many others on Malta.
- **PHILIP** ministered healing to many paralytics and lame people in Samaria.
- **THE APOSTLES** regularly laid hands on the sick and saw them recover.

Modern Application

In our medicalized world that often separates physical healing from spiritual wholeness, the gift of healing demonstrates God's concern for the complete person. Your gift serves as a tangible expression of God's compassion for those who suffer. Whether praying for physical ailments, emotional wounds, spiritual oppression, or relational brokenness, you become a conduit of God's restoring power. This gift isn't about techniques or formulas—it's about being available to the Holy Spirit in the moment, following His lead as He works through you to manifest Jesus' healing ministry today.

Gift in Action

THE SETTING: During a church gathering, you notice someone exhibiting signs of physical pain or discomfort.

HEALING RESPONSE: You feel a specific prompting from the Holy Spirit regarding their condition, perhaps even sensing exactly where or how they're hurting. With permission, you pray with authority, perhaps laying hands on them as the Spirit leads.

You might say: "I believe God wants to touch your [specific area] right now. May I pray for you? Father, in Jesus' name, I speak healing to this shoulder. Pain, go now. Muscles and tendons, be restored to full function. I thank you, Lord, that your healing power is flowing right now."

Power Combinations

- **HEALING + KNOWLEDGE** = Divine insight directing precisely targeted healing prayer
- **HEALING + FAITH** = Unwavering confidence that empowers bold healing ministry
- **HEALING + MERCY** = Compassionate healing touch that ministers to the whole person

Reflection Questions

1. How has God used you to minister healing to others in the past?
2. What physical sensations or spiritual impressions typically accompany your healing ministry?
3. How do you maintain faith when healing manifestation is delayed or different than expected?
4. What barriers might be preventing you from stepping more fully into this gift?

Holistic Healing?

Healing obviously refers to removing diseases from the spirit, soul, or body. Most of us can quickly think of diseases of the body, but diseases of the spirit, such as bitterness, greed, and guilt, can also be healed by the power of God. Some of the diseases of the soul are discouragement, worry, jealousy, fear, anxiety, and other destructive dispositions.

MIRACLES

The divine ability to alter the natural outcomes of life in a supernatural way through prayer, faith, and divine direction.

> In some translations, Paul names this gift "the gift of working miracles." The word working is a translation of the Greek word *energema*, which Strong's Concordance defines simply as "an effect." The "works of miracles" are a translation of the Greek word *dunamis*, which means "specifically miraculous power (usually by implication a miracle itself)."[19]

Scripture Foundation

"To another the working of miracles..." (1 Corinthians 12:10)

Additional References: Acts 9:36–42, 19:11–12, 20:7–12; Romans 15:18–19; 1 Corinthians 12:10, 28

You Might Have This Gift If...

- You experience unusual boldness to pray for seemingly impossible interventions.
- You've witnessed supernatural events that defy natural explanation through your ministry.
- You're drawn to situations where only a divine intervention can solve the problem.
- You experience a special anointing in crisis situations requiring immediate divine help.
- You have unwavering confidence in God's power to do the extraordinary.
- You often sense a clear, specific direction from God about miraculous intervention.
- You're not intimidated by circumstances that have no logical solution.
- You've seen God work in ways that left no doubt about His supernatural involvement.
- You're often the one who prays when others feel a situation is hopeless.

Watch Out For...

- **MIRACLE-CHASING**—Signs follow the message; they aren't meant to replace it.
- **PRIDE IN POWER**—Remember that miracles manifest God's glory, not human importance.
- **SENSATIONALISM**—Authentic miracles don't need dramatic presentation.
- **NEGLECTING THE ORDINARY**—God often works through both miraculous and natural means.

Strengthen This Gift By...

- **BOLD OBEDIENCE**—Step out immediately when God prompts, despite fear or uncertainty.
- **SCRIPTURE IMMERSION**—Study biblical miracles to understand God's patterns.
- **SPIRITUAL AUTHORITY**—Grow in your understanding of your position in Christ.
- **FAITH COMMUNITY**—Connect with others who affirm and help steward this gift.

Biblical Examples

- **ELIJAH** called down fire from heaven on Mount Carmel.
- **PETER** raised Tabitha from the dead in Joppa.
- **PAUL** was unharmed by a venomous snakebite on Malta.
- **MOSES** parted the Red Sea with his staff at God's command.

Modern Application

In our naturalistic, skeptical age, miraculous interventions dramatically demonstrate that the living God still acts in human affairs. Your gift serves as a powerful apologetic for the gospel. Whether commanding nature (weather, elements, etc.), experiencing supernatural protection, witnessing creative miracles (restoration of missing functions or parts), or seeing divine interventions that defy natural law, you demonstrate that Jesus remains "the same yesterday, today, and forever" (Hebrews 13:8). This gift isn't about spectacle or attention—it's about revealing God's kingdom power in situations where human ability has reached its limit.

Gift in Action

THE SETTING: A critical ministry situation arises in which only supernatural intervention can overcome an obstacle, such as desperate financial need, dangerous environmental conditions, or a logistical impossibility.

MIRACLES RESPONSE: While others focus on human solutions or resign themselves to failure, you feel a divine conviction to exercise spiritual authority over the situation. With bold faith, you speak directly to the mountain, commanding it to move in Jesus' name.

You might say: "In the authority of Jesus Christ, I command this storm to dissipate now. Winds, be still. Clouds, disperse. I declare that God's purpose will not be hindered, and His people will proceed safely to accomplish His will."

Power Combinations

- **MIRACLES + EVANGELISM** = Supernatural signs that confirm the gospel message
- **MIRACLES + APOSTLESHIP** = Kingdom breakthrough in pioneer territory
- **MIRACLES + DISCERNMENT** = Power ministry guided by spiritual sensitivity

Reflection Questions

1. When have you witnessed or been part of a genuine miracle that had no natural explanation?
2. What obstacles to belief tend to diminish your expectation for miraculous intervention?
3. In what current impossible situation might God be calling you to exercise supernatural authority?
4. How does your understanding of God's character influence your confidence in miraculous power?

Do Miracles Still Happen?

The definition implies no boundaries or limitations, which is appropriate, since the power of our mighty God has none. Miracles do still happen today, most of us just don't recognize them. We assume the only miracles are when the waters part, not when marriages are miraculously reconciled. Our modern culture downplays the supernatural; therefore, we don't recognize or expect it to happen often.

Based on the definitions of the Greek words mentioned at the beginning of this section, I believe that the supernatural gift of miracles is used to serve others as an expression of God's miracle-working power.

PROPHECY

> NOTE: The "Prophecy" gift is repeated in the Motivational Gifts, Ministry Gifts, and Manifestation Gifts sections. Although there may be slight variations in the use and function of this gift based on biblical scholars' understanding of the roles associated with it, it retains the same foundational characteristics. For this reason, the following definition and support Scripture are repeated in all three gifts sections.

The divine strength to communicate God's truth in a way that calls people to a right relationship with God.

Scripture Foundation

> *"But everyone who prophesies speaks to people for their strengthening, encouraging and comfort." (1 Corinthians 14:3)*

Additional References: Acts 2:37–40, 7:51–53, 26:24–29; 1 Thessalonians 1:5

Prophecy is an English word derived from the Greek word *propheteia,* as used by Paul in his letter to the Corinthians. *Propheteia* is translated as either *prophecy* or *prophesying* throughout the New Testament, and Strong's Concordance best defines it as "prediction (scriptural or other)."[20]

You Might Have This Gift If...

- You're wired with a strong sense of right and wrong that feels almost like a spiritual compass.

- You see the world in clear moral terms rather than shades of gray.
- You find yourself unable to compromise on deeply-held convictions, even when it would be easier.
- You often feel a holy urgency to challenge destructive patterns in others' lives.
- People describe you as "principled" or say you have "strong convictions."
- You're willing to stand firm for truth even when it makes you unpopular.
- You naturally filter situations through "What does God's Word say about this?"
- You feel a deep responsibility to speak truth, even when others remain silent.

Watch Out For...

- **TRUTH WITHOUT LOVE**—Remember, prophecy without love is just noise (1 Cor. 13:2).
- **JUDGMENT VS. DISCERNMENT**—Be careful not to condemn people while confronting actions.
- **TIMING MATTERS**—Even a perfect truth delivered at the wrong time can be rejected.
- **THE MESSENGER'S HEART**—Check your motives: Are you speaking to build up or to prove you're right?

Strengthen This Gift By...

- **SCRIPTURE IMMERSION**—Your prophetic gift is most powerful when aligned with God's written Word.

- **PRACTICING COMPASSION**—Intentionally see the person behind the behavior you're addressing.
- **SEEKING FEEDBACK**—Ask trusted friends if your delivery matches your heart.
- **PRAYER PARTNERSHIP**—Find prayer partners who will cover you when you exercise this gift.

Biblical Examples

- **NATHAN** confronted King David with "You are the man!" after his sin with Bathsheba.
- **ESTHER** risked everything to speak truth to power: "If I perish, I perish."
- **JOHN THE BAPTIST** fearlessly called people to repentance and preparation.
- **PAUL** addressed the Athenians by connecting to their cultural understanding before delivering the truth.

Modern Application

The prophetic voice today speaks God's unchanging truth into our changing world. Whether addressing social justice issues, calling out corruption in systems, or confronting personal sin in love, prophetic people pull back the curtain on what's really happening beneath the surface. Your gift helps others see situations as God sees them.

While the Old Testament prophets often predicted future events, today's prophetic gift primarily forth-tells (speaks God's truth) rather than foretells (predicts future events).

Gift in Action

THE SETTING: Your small group is discussing a popular self-help book that subtly contradicts biblical teaching.

PROPHETIC RESPONSE: While others focus on the helpful elements, you sense something isn't right. Instead of dismissing the entire book or attacking those who like it, you thoughtfully identify specific points that contradict Scripture, helping the group discern truth from error.

You might say: "I appreciate how this book helps people take responsibility for their lives, but I'm concerned about the way it defines success primarily through achievement rather than Christ-likeness. What if we examined these principles through a biblical filter?"

Power Combinations

- **PROPHECY + MERCY** = Truth delivered with remarkable compassion
- **PROPHECY + TEACHING** = Biblical principles explained with conviction and clarity
- **PROPHECY + ENCOURAGEMENT** = Truth that inspires positive action rather than shame

Reflection Questions

1. When was the last time you felt compelled to speak truth when others remained silent?
2. How has God used your straightforward perspective to help others see situations more clearly?

> 3. In what areas might God be calling you to develop more grace in your truth-telling?
> 4. What truth do you sense God asking you to speak right now? To whom? How?

Future-tellers?

Let's add some clarity to what many believe is the gifting (or office) of prophecy. The prophets of the Old Testament had a remarkable gift and duty to speak the Word of God to His people, and to foretell events and outcomes based on what they heard from God. This is similar to how the Gift of prophecy works today, except that we (followers of Christ) now have God's Word given to us through the Holy Spirit's inspiration of the written Scriptures.

"The work of the Old-Testament prophets was not only to foretell future things, but to warn the people concerning sin and duty, and to be their remembrancers concerning that which they knew before. And thus gospel preachers are prophets, and do indeed, as far as the revelation of the word goes, foretell things to come."[21]

"Those with the gift of prophecy speak the truth of God's Word under the guidance of the Holy Spirit."[22]

This is not to say that those with a specific mixture of gifts (discernment, special knowledge) won't combine them with their gift of prophecy to proclaim Truth with a supernatural understanding of something that we could not ordinarily know (special knowledge) or see in our present state (discernment). When we consider these gift mixes, we understand how one might confuse the gift of prophecy with the Old Testament calling (and office) of a Prophet. While the powerful gift of prophecy remains, the office of a future-telling intermediary on God's behalf does not.

- When exercising your gift of prophecy, speak it boldly with Scriptural wisdom. All prophecy from God will align with God's written Word. Allow space for the Holy Spirit to confirm the word of prophecy you share with someone in their hearts. Be cautious of assigning or insinuating a timeline of your prophecy unless it's supported within the written Word of God.
- When receiving a word of prophecy from someone, use Scriptural wisdom in receiving it. Does it align with the Truth of God's Word? Be cautious of what is claimed as a "new revelation." Has the Holy Spirit within given you peace and confirmation? Is there a timeline insinuated, and if so, are you able to discern if that timing is from God or from the giver of that prophecy?

DISCERNMENT OF SPIRITS

The divine ability to distinguish between divine, human, and demonic sources behind words, actions, or spiritual manifestations.

In 1 Corinthians 12:10, the word *discerning* is a translation of the Greek word *diakrisis*, which means "judicial estimation." The word *spirits* is a translation of the Greek word *pneuma*, which means "a current of air, i.e., breath (blast) or a breeze; by analogy or figuratively, a spirit, an angel, demon, or (divine) God, Christ's spirit, the Holy Spirit."[23]

Scripture Foundation

"To another distinguishing between spirits..." (1 Corinthians 12:10).

Additional References: Matthew 16:21–23; Acts 5:1–11, 16:16–18; 1 Corinthians 12:10; 1 John 4:1–6

You Might Have This Gift If...

- You can often sense the source of spiritual activity or manifestation.
- You have an unusual sensitivity to authenticity and falsehood in spiritual matters.
- You can identify mixed motives or spiritual manipulation that others miss.
- You regularly sense when something is "off," even when everything appears fine on the surface.
- You experience physical or spiritual reactions to certain environments or teachings.
- You can recognize the root of spiritual oppression in people's lives.
- You naturally test teachings and practices against Scripture.
- You can often perceive whether behavior stems from psychological, spiritual, or physical sources.
- You have an internal alarm system that activates around counterfeit spirituality.

Watch Out For...

- **SUSPICION VS. DISCERNMENT**—True discernment comes from the Spirit, not cynicism.
- **JUDGMENTALISM**—The purpose is protection and freedom, not condemnation.
- **ISOLATION**—This gift can be isolating if you see what others don't.
- **FEAR-BASED MINISTRY**—Discernment should lead to freedom, not fear or demon-hunting.

Strengthen This Gift By...

- **BIBLICAL LITERACY**—Develop deep knowledge of Scripture as your testing standard.
- **PRAYER CULTIVATION**—Sharpen your spiritual sensitivity through consistent prayer.
- **BALANCED COMMUNITY**—Stay connected with mature believers who provide perspective.
- **PRACTICAL APPLICATION**—Learn how to appropriately respond to what you discern.

Biblical Examples

- **PETER** discerned the deception in Ananias and Sapphira's hearts.
- **PAUL** identified a demonic spirit in the fortune-telling slave girl at Philippi.
- **JOHN** encouraged testing the spirits to see if they acknowledge Christ.

- **JESUS** recognized when Peter's words came from Satan rather than God.

Modern Application

In our spiritually confused culture, where truth and deception often appear intermingled, discernment of spirits provides essential protection. Your gift helps maintain spiritual integrity and safety. Whether identifying false teaching that subtly distorts truth, recognizing spiritual oppression requiring specific prayer, discerning hidden agendas behind spiritual facades, or distinguishing between divine guidance and counterfeit leading, you serve as a crucial guardian. This gift isn't about being spiritually suspicious—it's about seeing clearly in realms where others may be spiritually nearsighted, helping the body of Christ navigate safely through increasingly deceptive times.

Gift in Action

THE SETTING: Your church community is enthusiastically embracing a new teaching or practice that feels spiritually questionable to you despite its apparent positive results.

DISCERNMENT RESPONSE: Rather than making accusatory statements, you prayerfully examine the specific elements causing concern and test them against Scripture. You then share your insights with appropriate leadership in a constructive way.

You might say: "I've been praying about this new teaching, and while I see why it's appealing, I'm discerning some concerning elements at its foundation. When we trace these ideas back to their source, they seem to contradict these specific Scriptures. Could we take some time to carefully examine this together?"

Power Combinations

- **DISCERNMENT + WISDOM** = Spiritual insight paired with divine guidance on proper response
- **DISCERNMENT + TEACHING** = Clear instruction that separates truth from subtle error
- **DISCERNMENT + PROPHECY** = Revelation that addresses hidden spiritual dynamics

Reflection Questions

1. When have you sensed something was spiritually "off" that later proved accurate?
2. How does God typically alert you to spiritual deception or danger?
3. What challenges have you experienced in appropriately responding to what you discern?
4. How might God be calling you to serve as a spiritual guardian in your current context?

Judge Much?

Discernment rides a fine line between judgment and understanding. It is paramount for the person who works within this gift to never yield to human reasoning and to condemn others through self-righteous judgment. The weighing of information and motives to bring understanding and clarity gives the gifted person an opportunity to challenge, rebuke, and encourage another believer with the truth of God's Word.

TONGUES

The divine ability to speak in a language unknown to the speaker, whether an unlearned human language or a heavenly language.

> The English "words of tongues" are a translation of the Greek word *glossa*, which Strong's Concordance defines as "the tongue; by implication a language (specifically one naturally unacquired)." Throughout the New Testament, *glossa* is translated only as tongue (singular or plural). Therefore, we could say that "diverse kinds of tongues" refers to "kindred languages that are not naturally acquired."[24]

Scripture Foundation

"To another different kinds of tongues, and to another the interpretation of tongues" (1 Corinthians 12:10).

Additional References: Acts 2:1–13, 10:44–46, 19:1–7; 1 Corinthians 12:10, 28, 14:1–40

You Might Have This Gift If...

- You experience the Holy Spirit prompting you to pray or speak in an unknown language.
- You find your spirit strengthened and refreshed when praying in tongues.
- You've spoken words you didn't understand that others recognized as a known language.

- You sense a deeper communion with God when praying in a language beyond your natural one.
- You occasionally receive interpretations of your or others' tongues.
- You experience a breakthrough in intercession when praying in the Spirit.
- You find yourself worshiping in tongues during times of intimate communion with God.
- You've observed supernatural impact when speaking in tongues in appropriate settings.
- You've experienced increased spiritual sensitivity after praying in tongues.

Watch Out For...

- **ELEVATION ABOVE OTHER GIFTS**—Tongues is valuable but not superior to other manifestations.
- **CONFUSION IN CORPORATE SETTINGS**—Public tongues should follow biblical guidelines (1 Cor. 14).
- **ARTIFICIAL MANIFESTATION**—True tongues flow from the Spirit, not human imitation.
- **PRIDEFUL DISPLAY**—The purpose is edification, not spiritual showmanship.

Strengthen This Gift By...

- **PRIVATE CULTIVATION**—Develop this gift primarily in your personal prayer life.

- **BIBLICAL UNDERSTANDING**—Study Scripture's teaching on the proper use of tongues.
- **SEEKING INTERPRETATION**—Pray for interpretation when using tongues in corporate settings.
- **SENSITIVITY TO CONTEXT**—Learn when and how this gift is most appropriately expressed.

Biblical Examples

- **THE DISCIPLES** at Pentecost spoke in languages they hadn't learned.
- **CORNELIUS' HOUSEHOLD** spontaneously spoke in tongues when the Spirit fell.
- **THE EPHESIAN BELIEVERS** spoke in tongues when Paul laid hands on them.
- **PAUL** himself prayed in tongues frequently in his private devotion.

Modern Application

In our cognitively dominated culture, tongues remind us that communication with God transcends intellectual limits. Your gift provides access to prayer beyond human understanding. Whether praying in a heavenly language that bypasses cognitive limitations, speaking in an unlearned human language as a sign to unbelievers, expressing worship that transcends natural vocabulary, or delivering a corporate message requiring interpretation, you demonstrate that the Spirit still empowers communication beyond natural capacity. This gift isn't about ecstatic emotional display—it's about the Spirit praying through you "with groans that words cannot express" (Romans

8:26), often addressing matters too deep or complex for natural language.

Gift in Action

THE SETTING: During intense personal prayer for a complex situation where you don't know how to pray effectively, or in a corporate worship setting where the Spirit prompts supernatural expression.

TONGUES RESPONSE: You yield to the Holy Spirit's prompting, allowing Him to pray through you in a language you haven't learned. In private, this flows freely; in public settings, you follow biblical guidelines for order and interpretation.

In private, you simply yield: "Holy Spirit, I don't know how to pray about this situation. I invite you to pray through me according to the Father's perfect will."

In public, you might say (if appropriate in your context): "I believe the Spirit is giving me a message in tongues. I'll share it and then wait for interpretation before we proceed, as Scripture instructs."

Power Combinations

- **TONGUES + INTERPRETATION** = Supernatural message delivered with divine understanding
- **TONGUES + INTERCESSION** = Spirit-empowered prayer that transcends human limitations
- **TONGUES + WORSHIP** = Supernatural expression of adoration beyond natural language

> **Reflection Questions**
>
> 1. How has praying in tongues impacted your personal communion with God?
> 2. What differences do you notice in your spiritual life when you regularly exercise this gift versus when you don't?
> 3. What questions or uncertainties do you still have about this gift and its proper expression?
> 4. How might God be inviting you to grow in both your understanding and exercise of this gift?

Why the Controversy?

Perhaps more than any others, the spiritual gifts of tongues and interpretation of tongues have been confused and misunderstood among believers. Paul even had to address it in 1 Corinthians 14 to help the church understand the purpose and use of tongues. It is important to remember that all of the gifts are inexplicable in natural terms. They are supernatural gifts. We should study what the Scriptures say about these gifts and trust God to direct them according to His will. As the Holy Spirit gives these gifts, believers are equipped to serve others and glorify God.

Modern-day use and understanding of this gift should be approached with faith. There are modern-day testimonies of this gift being used properly and of God being glorified in it, as well as of it being abused for man's edification.

There are several purposes listed for the use of the gift of tongues.

1. Worship, praise, and prayer (Jude 20:21)
2. Encouraging other believers (1 Corinthians 14:) (Note: Requires someone with the gift of Interpretation of Tongues to edify the church at large.)
3. A sign to unbelievers (1 Corinthians 14:22)

The gift was essentially an ecstatic utterance of highly wrought emotion that edified the speaker (1 John 14:4) and was intelligible to God (1 John 14:2; 1 John 14:28). It was not always true that the speaker in tongues could make clear what he had said to those who did not know the tongue (1 John 14:13). It was a real language that could be understood by one familiar with that tongue as was seen on the great Day of Pentecost when people who spoke different languages were present.[25]

INTERPRETATION OF TONGUES

The divine ability to reveal the meaning of a message given in tongues for the edification of the hearers.

> The word "interpretation" is a translation of the Greek word *hermeneia*, which is defined simply as "translation." The word tongues that is used in this phrase is another instance in which the Greek word *glossa* ("the tongue") is used. "Interpretation of tongues" could be paraphrased as "translation of languages that have not been naturally acquired."[26]

Scripture Foundation

"To another the interpretation of tongues" (1 Corinthians 12:10).

Additional References: Acts 2:1–13; 1 Corinthians 12:10, 14:5, 13, 26–28

You Might Have This Gift If...

- You receive divine understanding of messages given in unknown languages.
- You experience a supernatural ability to translate what others have spoken in tongues.
- You find meaning arising in your spirit when tongues are spoken.
- You've accurately conveyed the heart of a tongues message that was later confirmed.
- You feel especially prompted to respond when tongues are expressed in corporate settings.
- You receive not just a literal translation but the essence and spirit of a tongue's message.
- You sense a special responsibility toward maintaining order in the exercise of tongues.
- You find yourself receiving interpretation even when not expected.
- You experience a deep resonance with certain tongues' messages but not others.

Watch Out For...

- **FORCED INTERPRETATION**—True interpretation flows from the Spirit, not human effort.
- **MESSAGE MANIPULATION**—Faithfully deliver what God reveals, not personal additions.
- **CONFUSION BETWEEN INTERPRETATION AND PROPHECY**—Though related, they're distinct gifts.
- **BYPASSING CHURCH ORDER**—Work within biblical guidelines for corporate expression.

Strengthen This Gift By...

- **SPIRITUAL RECEPTIVITY**—Cultivate sensitivity to the Spirit's voice and promptings.
- **BIBLICAL UNDERSTANDING**—Study Scripture's teaching on proper use of interpretation.
- **ACCOUNTABILITY RELATIONSHIPS**—Submit your interpretations to mature spiritual oversight.
- **PAIRED MINISTRY**—Work cooperatively with those who have the gift of tongues.

Biblical Examples

- **THE PENTECOST HEARERS** each heard the disciples speaking in their own native language.
- **THE CORINTHIAN CHURCH** had guidelines for the interpretation accompanying tongues.

- **PAUL'S TEACHING** emphasized interpretation for public edification.
- **EARLY CHURCH PRACTICE** included both tongues and interpretation in orderly worship.

Modern Application

In our individualistic culture that often struggles with spiritual community, the interpretation of tongues reinforces our interconnectedness. Your gift transforms potentially isolating spiritual experiences into communal edification. Whether translating a public tongues message for corporate understanding, providing interpretation that confirms personal guidance, bridging cultural and linguistic divides in ministry contexts, or helping maintain biblical order in charismatic expression, you demonstrate that the Spirit gives gifts for mutual benefit, not individual experience. This gift isn't about demonstrating spiritual prowess—it's about ensuring that supernatural communication accomplishes its purpose of building up the body of Christ.

Gift in Action

THE SETTING: During a corporate gathering, someone appropriately delivers a message in tongues according to biblical guidelines, and there is a holy pause awaiting interpretation.

INTERPRETATION RESPONSE: You sense the Spirit giving you understanding of the message, not necessarily word-for-word translation, but the heart and meaning of what was expressed.

You might say: "I believe the interpretation of this message is: 'My children, I see your weariness in this season of waiting.

What appears as a delay in your eyes is actually my perfect preparation. Do not measure my faithfulness by your timeline. I am working beneath the surface in ways your eyes cannot yet perceive. Hold fast your confidence, for the fulfillment is nearer than you realize.'"

Power Combinations

- **INTERPRETATION + PROPHECY** = Divine understanding that expands into prophetic application
- **INTERPRETATION + WISDOM** = Supernatural translation paired with insight for application
- **INTERPRETATION + FAITH** = Confident delivery that strengthens corporate belief

Reflection Questions

1. When have you experienced receiving an interpretation that you knew came from beyond your understanding?
2. How does interpretation typically come to you—through words, impressions, pictures, or other means?
3. What has helped you distinguish between true spiritual interpretation and your own thoughts or desires?
4. How might God be calling you to responsibly develop this gift for the benefit of your community?

This gift is often paired with speaking in unknown languages or is used in conjunction with it. There are many testimonies of missionaries who have visited tribes speaking a language they did not know but were gifted by God to begin immediately understanding that language.

This also applies to understanding what is being prayed for in a heavenly language. Since only God can validate these gifts, we believe both can be a correct understanding of them.

The purpose of this gift is to edify the body of Christ. *"So anyone who speaks in tongues should pray also for the ability to interpret what has been said."* (1 Corinthians 14:13)

A Word About Manifestation Gifts

These nine gifts aren't spiritual curiosities or ancient relics—they're vital expressions of the Holy Spirit's continuing work among us. They aren't reserved for spiritual superstars or professional ministers; they're distributed throughout the body of Christ "just as He determines" (1 Corinthians 12:11).

Some manifestation gifts may operate consistently in your life, while others may emerge in specific seasons or situations as needed. The key isn't seeking the gifts themselves but cultivating intimacy with the Giver, who distributes them according to His wisdom and purpose.

Remember the Apostle Paul's wisdom: pursue love first, then eagerly desire spiritual gifts, especially those that build up the church (1 Corinthians 14:1). As you surrender yourself fully to God's purposes, you'll find Him working through you in ways that continually amaze and humble you—often when you least expect it.

These gifts were given to you on purpose FOR purpose. They aren't meant to draw attention to you but to manifest the continuing presence and power of Jesus in a world desperate for supernatural reality. Use them faithfully, humbly, and biblically—and watch what God will do!

*Additional Resources Used in Gifts Codex [27] [28]

PART 3
Living GIFTED

10

MYTHS AND MISCONCEPTIONS: CLEARING THE PATH TO YOUR PURPOSE

Have you ever noticed how a small pebble in your shoe can completely derail a journey? It's not the mountain ahead that stops you—it's that tiny hindrance with every step.

That's what misconceptions about spiritual gifts do. They're not massive theological barriers; they're those nagging little distortions that create just enough friction to keep us from walking fully in our divine design. And friend, the enemy of your soul is perfectly content with you identifying your gifts as long as misunderstanding keeps you from actually using them.

I've watched it happen countless times—believers who glimpse their giftedness but remain paralyzed by subtle lies they've absorbed without even realizing it. The prophet who stays silent because she fears being labeled "weird." The mercy-giver who burns out because he believes boundaryless sacrifice is spiritual maturity. The teacher downplays her insight by saying, "Anyone could explain this."

These aren't just harmless confusions; they're strategic roadblocks that have kept God's people functioning at a fraction of their capacity for generations.

In this chapter, we're going to pull those pebbles from your shoes. We'll examine the most common misconceptions about each spiritual gift—not just for academic clarity, but for your liberation. When we identify and dismantle these distortions, something remarkable happens: Gifts that have been lying dormant suddenly spring to life. Limitations you thought were personality flaws reveal themselves as simply misinterpreted potential.

As we explore each gift, I invite you to ask the Holy Spirit to highlight areas where you've accepted lies as truth. Let Him gently expose the misconceptions that have limited your expression. Allow Him to replace confusion with clarity.

The path to walking on purpose FOR purpose requires clearing away the debris of misinformation. It demands looking honestly at what we've been taught—or absorbed through observation—and holding it up against the truth of Scripture and the heart of God.

Ready to remove those pebbles from your shoes? Let's begin the journey toward unleashing your gifts without the hindrance of misunderstanding.

PROPHECY

MYTH #1: *"Prophecy is primarily about predicting the future."*

TRUTH: While prophecy can include foretelling, it's primarily about "forth-telling" God's heart for the present moment. Most prophetic ministry involves speaking timely truth, encouragement, or direction that people need right now. Think of it this way: When a doctor gives a prognosis, it's based on what they diagnose in the present. Similarly, biblical prophecy often addresses current heart conditions and points to their natural outcomes if left unchanged.

MYTH #2: *"You need a title or platform to be prophetic."*

TRUTH: Some of the most powerful prophetic moments happen in everyday conversations, not from stages or pulpits. That whispered word of encouragement that uncannily addresses someone's deepest struggle? That's prophecy in action. God doesn't need spotlights to speak through you—just availability. The question isn't whether you have a prophetic title, but whether you're willing to deliver heaven's mail when God hands you an envelope with someone's name on it.

MYTH #3: *"If my prophetic word doesn't come true, I wasn't hearing from God."*

TRUTH: Prophecy isn't fortune-telling; it's partnering with a relational God. Some prophetic words are conditional, some involve human response, and yes, sometimes we filter divine impressions through our own expectations or misinterpretations. This doesn't make you a false prophet; it makes you a growing one. Remember when Nathan told David he should build the temple, only to return later with a correction? Even established prophets are learning to steward this gift. Humility and accountability are your greatest allies in prophetic development.

SERVING

MYTH #1: *"The gift of serving is just for people who aren't qualified for more visible ministry."*

TRUTH: Serving isn't the consolation prize of spiritual gifts—it's the foundation that makes all other ministries possible. Jesus himself defined His entire purpose as "not to be served, but to serve" (Mark 10:45). If serving was Jesus' primary mode of ministry, how dare we consider it secondary? The server with pure motives might be the most Christlike person in your church, regardless of who's behind the microphone.

MYTH #2: *"Anyone can serve; it's not really a special gift."*

TRUTH: While all Christians are called to serve, those with this gift have a supernatural capacity, consistency, and creativity in meeting needs. They see practical gaps others miss and derive genuine joy from filling them. It's the difference between someone who reluctantly helps when directly asked versus the person who shows up with exactly what's needed before anyone realizes there was a lack. Don't diminish what God has supernaturally empowered within you because it seems "ordinary."

MYTH #3: *"The gift of serving is just about doing physical tasks."*

TRUTH: This gift manifests in countless ways beyond setting up chairs or preparing meals. I've known gifted servers who serve through meticulous research, creating systems that multiply ministry effectiveness, or developing resources that equip others. Your serving gift might express itself through technology, administration, or creative problem-solving. The question isn't what tasks you perform, but whether you're supernaturally equipped to remove obstacles so others can flourish.

TEACHING

MYTH #1: *"You need formal education to have a teaching gift."*

TRUTH: While education can sharpen this gift, many powerful teachers have little formal training. The gift isn't about credentials; it's about a God-given ability to make truth clear and applicable. Some of the most effective Bible teachers I know never set foot in seminary, yet they can illuminate Scripture in ways that transform lives. What matters is your commitment to handling God's Word accurately and your supernatural ability to help others grasp and apply it.

MYTH #2: *"The teaching gift is mainly for explaining information."*

TRUTH: True teaching isn't simply transferring information—it's facilitating transformation. You're not just filling heads with facts; you're cultivating hearts that respond to truth. Jesus rarely taught through lectures. He used questions, stories, and real-life situations to help truth take root in His hearers' lives. If people walk away from your teaching knowing more but living no differently, you've informed them but not truly taught them.

MYTH #3: *"You need to be charismatic and dynamic to be an effective teacher."*

TRUTH: Teaching styles are as diverse as the teachers themselves. Some are animated storytellers; others are thoughtful, systematic thinkers. Some connect through humor; others through depth. The power of your teaching comes from the Spirit working through your authentic voice, not your ability to mimic someone else's style. God designed your specific personality as the perfect delivery system for the truths He wants to communicate through you. Don't try to be Beth Moore if God made you Max Lucado!

GIVING

MYTH #1: *"The gift of giving is only for wealthy people."*

TRUTH: This gift isn't measured by the size of your bank account but by your supernatural joy and discernment in stewarding resources for Kingdom impact. Some of the most gifted givers I know have modest incomes but extraordinary vision for how their resources can advance God's purposes. Remember the widow Jesus commended? She gave from her poverty, yet Jesus highlighted her gift above all others. It's not about how much you have; it's about how God has wired you to view and deploy what He's entrusted to you.

MYTH #2: *"Giving is just about money."*

TRUTH: Those with this gift often give generously across multiple dimensions: their time, talents, connections, influence, possessions, and yes, finances. You might express this gift by opening your home, sharing your expertise, lending your resources, or connecting people to opportunities. The essence of this gift is a supernatural generosity that flows from recognizing that everything you have belongs to God and is available for His purposes.

MYTH #3: *"If I'm not giving to my church, I'm not using my giving gift."*

TRUTH: While tithing is a biblical principle for all believers, the gift of giving often expresses itself through strategic, Spirit-led giving to various Kingdom causes. Your church deserves your faithful support, but God may also direct your giving toward missions, community outreach, individuals in crisis, emerging ministries, or marketplace opportunities that advance His purposes. The question isn't whether you're giving to the "right" place, but whether you're sensitively following God's specific direction for your resources.

ENCOURAGEMENT

MYTH #1: *"Encouragement is just about making people feel good."*

TRUTH: While affirmation is part of encouragement, this gift goes much deeper than positive vibes. The Greek word *parakaleo* means "to call alongside"—it's about strengthening others to take their next step with God. Sometimes this means cheering achievements, but it equally includes challenging complacency, comforting in grief, or redirecting misguided efforts. True encouragement isn't about making people feel better; it's about helping them become better by infusing courage for their God-given journey.

MYTH #2: *"Encouragement is a 'soft' gift without real spiritual power."*

TRUTH: Don't be fooled by this gift's gentleness—it carries tremendous spiritual authority. Barnabas ("Son of Encouragement") shaped Christian history by believing in Paul when others feared him and later advocating for John Mark after his failure. His encouragement directly enabled two men who wrote much of the New Testament! In a world that constantly tears down, Spirit-empowered encouragement literally changes the trajectory of lives and ministries. Never underestimate the kingdom power of a timely word that puts courage back into a depleted heart.

MYTH #3: *"You don't need special discernment to encourage people."*

TRUTH: Generic affirmation ("You're awesome!") can momentarily lift spirits, but the true gift of encouragement involves supernatural insight into what someone specifically needs in their current battle. It's about discerning whether they need challenging or comforting, whether to address their potential or their progress, whether they need gentle reassurance or a loving push. The most powerful encouragement comes when the Holy Spirit gives you the exact words that address someone's unspoken fears or doubts. This isn't just being nice; it's being divinely strategic.

LEADERSHIP

MYTH #1: *"Leadership is about being in charge and making decisions."*

TRUTH: Biblical leadership isn't about position or control; it's about influence and service. Jesus explicitly contrasted worldly leadership ("lording it over others") with Kingdom leadership ("whoever wants to be great must become a servant"). True spiritual leadership isn't measured by how many people serve you, but by how effectively you equip and empower others. The question isn't whether people follow your commands, but whether they're becoming more like Jesus under your influence.

MYTH #2: *"You must be extroverted and charismatic to have leadership gifting."*

TRUTH: Leadership styles are beautifully diverse. Moses was "slow of speech," yet led millions. Deborah led through wisdom and conviction. Timothy led despite his youth and apparent timidity. God intentionally gifts different kinds of leaders because different seasons and contexts require different approaches. Some leaders inspire through vision, others through steady consistency. Some lead from the front, others from alongside. Don't dismiss your leadership gift because you don't fit cultural stereotypes.

MYTH #3: *"If no one has given me a leadership title, I don't have this gift."*

TRUTH: Titles confirm leadership; they don't create it. Leadership gifting reveals itself whenever you help others move from where they are to where God wants them to be—regardless of your formal position. You might be exercising leadership when mentoring one person, facilitating a small group, coordinating volunteers, or influencing organizational culture. Joseph led from a prison before he led from a palace. Focus less on acquiring leadership positions and more on faithfully stewarding the influence God has already given you.

MERCY

MYTH #1: *"Mercy is just being nice to people."*

TRUTH: The gift of mercy goes far beyond general kindness. It's a supernatural capacity to enter into others' pain without being destroyed by it, to stand in solidarity with the suffering when others can only offer quick solutions or platitudes. Those with this gift have a God-given ability to sit in the darkness with others until the light returns. It's not about being nice; it's about being present in a way that tangibly demonstrates God hasn't abandoned those who suffer.

MYTH #2: *"Showing mercy enables dysfunction and delays necessary change."*

TRUTH: Authentic mercy doesn't enable; it empowers. It doesn't ignore truth; it creates safe spaces for truth to be received. Jesus perfectly modeled this with the woman caught in adultery. He extended mercy that protected her dignity ("Neither do I condemn you") while still speaking truth that facilitated transformation ("Go and sin no more"). Those with this gift understand that mercy creates the relational trust needed for people to embrace difficult truths they might otherwise reject.

MYTH #3: *"Mercy is a one-dimensional gift that doesn't require wisdom or discernment."*

TRUTH: Effective mercy ministry requires remarkable wisdom to determine what form of compassion will truly help rather than harm. It requires discernment to address root causes rather than just symptoms. It requires boundaries to prevent compassion fatigue. The gift of mercy isn't just a sentimental heart response; it's a spiritually strategic approach to brokenness that aligns with God's redemptive purposes. The most effective mercy-givers are often profoundly discerning about what different situations require.

APOSTLE

MYTH #1: *"There are no apostles today; that gift ended with the early church."*

TRUTH: While the original twelve Apostles held a unique foundational role, the New Testament clearly shows others beyond the twelve who carried apostolic gifting (Paul, Barnabas, Andronicus, Junia, etc.). The gift continues today through those who establish new works, break into unreached territory, and set foundations for others to build upon. Modern apostolic gifting might express itself through church planting, pioneering new ministry models, reaching unreached people groups, or establishing kingdom influence in secular domains. The title may have changed, but the function remains vital.

MYTH #2: *"Apostolic gifting is about having authority over others."*

TRUTH: Paul described apostolic ministry as being "the very last, like men sentenced to death" (1 Cor. 4:9), and often emphasized his sacrifices rather than his authority. True apostolic gifting manifests as servant-leadership that empowers others rather than controls them. Those with this gift derive their greatest joy not from recognition but from seeing others succeed in what they've helped establish. Their authority comes not from titles but from spiritual fruitfulness and the willingness to pay prices others aren't willing to pay.

MYTH #3: *"Apostles are just highly successful entrepreneurs in church settings."*

TRUTH: While apostolic people often have entrepreneurial characteristics, this gift has distinct spiritual dimensions beyond business acumen. It includes supernatural breakthroughs in spiritual opposition, establishing Kingdom DNA in new ventures, and laying foundations aligned with heaven's blueprint rather than human innovation. Being a successful church-starter doesn't automatically indicate apostolic gifting—this gift specifically advances Christ's Kingdom according to divine strategy, not just human organizational skills.

EVANGELIST

MYTH #1: *"Evangelists are always extroverted and charismatic."*

TRUTH: The gift of evangelism comes in countless expressions. Some evangelists captivate crowds; others connect deeply in one-on-one conversations. Some are bold and direct; others are gentle and patient. Philip from Acts demonstrates both styles—preaching to crowds in Samaria but taking a measured, question-based approach with the Ethiopian official. Don't dismiss your evangelistic gifting because you don't fit the stereotype. The question isn't whether you have a particular personality but whether you carry a supernatural ability to help people understand and respond to the gospel.

MYTH #2: *"If you're not regularly leading people to Christ, you don't have an evangelistic gift."*

TRUTH: Even gifted evangelists experience seasons of planting without immediate harvesting. The effectiveness of this gift isn't measured solely by conversions but by faithfulness in clearly communicating the gospel, whether people respond immediately or not. Billy Graham preached for months without seeing a significant response before his breakthrough. Focus on faithfulness in sharing rather than immediate results—some evangelists specialize in sowing, others in watering, others in reaping, but God brings the increase (1 Cor. 3:6–7).

MYTH #3: *"Evangelists focus only on 'getting people saved' without discipleship."*

TRUTH: The healthiest expression of evangelistic gifting understands that the goal isn't merely decisions but disciples. In Matthew 28:19–20, Jesus commissioned us to "make disciples," not just converts. Many with this gift have developed remarkably effective approaches to helping new believers take their first steps in faith. Rather than separating evangelism and discipleship, see them as two sides of the same coin—introducing people to Jesus and helping them follow Him faithfully.

SHEPHERD

MYTH #1: *"The shepherding gift is just for those in pastoral ministry."*

TRUTH: While pastors certainly should have shepherding gifts, this gift expresses itself far beyond professional ministry. You might shepherd as a small group leader, mentor, ministry coordinator, parent, teacher, coach, manager, or friend. The essence of this gift isn't about position but about a supernatural capacity to nurture spiritual growth in others. Some of the most effective shepherds I know have never held a pastoral title but have profoundly shaped the spiritual journeys of countless people through their consistent care and guidance.

MYTH #2: *"Shepherding is mostly about offering comfort and care."*

TRUTH: Biblical shepherding includes both tender care and tough protection. David's shepherding involved both "leading beside still waters" and confronting lions and bears. Effective shepherds certainly provide compassionate care, but they also protect those in their care through appropriate boundaries, loving confrontation, and spiritual discernment about harmful influences. Don't confuse shepherding with mere niceness. Sometimes, the most loving act of a shepherd is to use their staff to pull someone back from spiritual danger.

MYTH #3: *"You need to be available 24/7 to be an effective shepherd."*

TRUTH: Even Jesus didn't make Himself constantly available to everyone. He often withdrew for prayer, set boundaries with crowds, and focused deeply on a smaller group rather than trying to personally shepherd everyone. Effective shepherds understand that sustainability requires boundaries, team approaches, and equipping others rather than doing all the ministry themselves. Your shepherding gift isn't meant to exhaust you but to flow through you as part of a larger body where others exercise their complementary gifts alongside yours.

WISDOM

MYTH #1: *"The gift of wisdom is just having good advice from life experience."*
TRUTH: While experience can certainly develop wisdom, the spiritual gift of wisdom involves supernatural insight that transcends human understanding. It's a divinely downloaded perspective that cuts through complexity with laser precision. This isn't accumulated knowledge or common sense—it's heaven's viewpoint breaking into earthly situations. Like when Solomon proposed dividing the baby, revealing the true mother's heart in a seemingly impossible case. This gift transcends natural wisdom, offering solutions and perspectives that can only come from God.

MYTH #2: *"Wisdom is primarily about having the right answers."*
TRUTH: Often, this gift manifests more through asking the right questions than giving quick answers. Jesus frequently responded to questions with deeper questions that shifted entire frameworks of understanding. Those with this gift often help others discover wisdom rather than simply dispensing it. They create space for reflection, reframe problems to reveal unseen dimensions, and guide people toward discovery rather than dependency. The highest expression of wisdom isn't making people reliant on your insights but helping them develop greater capacity for Spirit-led discernment themselves.

MYTH #3: *"The wisdom gift operates the same way in all situations."*
TRUTH: Divine wisdom is remarkably contextual, not formulaic. What constitutes wisdom in one situation might be

folly in another. Sometimes wisdom speaks boldly; other times it remains silent. Sometimes it takes decisive action; other times it patiently waits. Sometimes it provides clear solutions; other times it simply illuminates the right questions. Those with this gift learn to be deeply sensitive to the Spirit's direction, not just on what wisdom to share, but also on how and when to share it for maximum redemptive impact.

KNOWLEDGE

MYTH #1: *"Words of knowledge are just educated guesses or good intuition."*

TRUTH: While intuition and observation certainly have value, the gift of knowledge involves receiving specific information that couldn't be known through natural means. It's not clever deduction but divine revelation. Think of Jesus telling the Samaritan woman about her five husbands, or Peter knowing about Ananias and Sapphira's deception. This gift operates when God reveals facts, insights, or information that serve His redemptive purposes in a specific situation. It's not about being spiritually impressive but about demonstrating that God sees us intimately and cares about our specific circumstances.

MYTH #2: *"If I receive a word of knowledge, I should always share it immediately."*

TRUTH: Receiving divine information carries responsibility for how it's stewarded. Sometimes God reveals things for your prayer guidance rather than public disclosure. Sometimes timing and context matter greatly in how knowledge is shared. Sometimes the revelation requires additional confirmation before being delivered. Jesus knew all things but didn't always speak every truth He knew (John 16:12). Those with this gift learn to discern not just what God is revealing but why

He's revealing it and how He wants it handled in each unique situation.

MYTH #3: *"Words of knowledge will always be dramatic or obviously supernatural."*

TRUTH: While some expressions of this gift are undeniably supernatural, many come in seemingly ordinary impressions, thoughts, dreams, or Scriptures that suddenly stand out with unusual clarity. The supernatural element isn't necessarily in how the information arrives but in its pinpoint accuracy and redemptive impact. Don't dismiss quieter manifestations of this gift, or assume it operates only through dramatic revelations. God often whispers knowledge that He could shout, inviting our attentive partnership rather than passive observation.

FAITH

MYTH #1: *"The gift of faith is just about believing harder or having more confidence."*

TRUTH: This gift isn't about manufacturing stronger belief through human effort; it's a supernatural impartation of divine certainty. Those with this gift don't strain to believe; they receive confidence as a gift in specific situations. It's the difference between someone crossing a frozen lake because they've logically analyzed ice thickness (regular faith) versus someone who receives an unshakable knowing that crossing is safe despite apparent danger (gift of faith). This isn't positive thinking or blind optimism—it's divinely granted assurance that transcends both circumstances and the limits of normal faith.

MYTH #2: *"If you have enough faith, you'll never experience doubt or fear."*

TRUTH: Even those with remarkable faith gifts experience normal human emotions. The gift doesn't eliminate feelings; it provides supernatural certainty that operates alongside them. Smith Wigglesworth, known for extraordinary faith, admitted, "Fear knocked at the door, faith answered, and no one was there." The gift of faith isn't about never feeling afraid; it's about a God-given confidence that stands firm in the face of those feelings. Don't question your faith gift because you experience normal emotions—measure it by the supernatural certainty that remains when everything visible contradicts what God has spoken.

MYTH #3: *"The gift of faith is primarily for receiving personal miracles."*

TRUTH: While this gift certainly operates in believing for miraculous provision or intervention, it often functions most powerfully in kingdom advancement beyond personal needs. It's the supernatural confidence that enables pioneers to establish new works, reformers to challenge entrenched systems, intercessors to stand for breakthrough when all seems lost, and visionaries to pursue God-given dreams despite overwhelming odds. The gift often manifests most dramatically not in believing for personal blessing but in holding fast to God's purposes when everything visible suggests surrender would be wiser.

HEALING

MYTH #1: *"If you have the gift of healing, everyone you pray for will be healed."*

TRUTH: Even Jesus, who had the Spirit without measure, didn't heal everyone. In John 5, He healed only one man among many at the pool of Bethesda. This gift doesn't give us healing power independent of God's purposes and timing. Rather, it positions us as vessels through whom God's healing flows according to His sovereign wisdom. The effectiveness of this gift isn't measured by a 100% success rate but by faithful availability and supernatural results beyond what would happen naturally. Don't let imperfect results cause you to question your gift—focus instead on obedient response to God's healing prompts.

MYTH #2: *"The gift of healing is only about physical ailments."*

TRUTH: Biblical healing encompasses restoration of the whole person—body, soul, and spirit. Those with this gift may be especially effective in ministering emotional healing from trauma, spiritual healing from bondage, relational healing from brokenness, or mental healing from destructive thought patterns. All these dimensions reflect God's redemptive work. Some with this gift specialize in particular types of healing based on how God has uniquely wired and experienced them. Don't limit your understanding of this gift to just physical conditions—God's healing work is comprehensive.

MYTH #3: *"Modern medicine makes the gift of healing unnecessary."*

TRUTH: God often works through both natural and supernatural means. Medicine and miraculous healing aren't competitors but partners in God's redemptive purposes. Luke was both a physician and a witness to supernatural healing. Those with this gift recognize that God created scientific healing processes and also intervenes supernaturally—sometimes working through medical treatment, sometimes despite its limitations, sometimes alongside it. The question isn't whether God will heal through medicine OR miracle, but how He's choosing to work in each specific situation for maximum glory and good.

MIRACLES

MYTH #1: *"Real miracles only happened in biblical times."*

TRUTH: The same Jesus who said "the works that I do shall you do also, and greater works than these" (John 14:12) hasn't changed His mind about empowering His church. While miracles aren't evenly distributed across history or geography, credible documentation exists of genuine miraculous phenomena that have continued throughout church history into the present day. From creative provision to supernatural protection, from dramatic physical healings to extraordinary natural interventions, the gift of miracles continues to operate wherever faith creates space for God's supernatural power to manifest through yielded vessels.

MYTH #2: *"Miracles should be commonplace for Spirit-filled believers."*

TRUTH: Even in Scripture, miracles weren't everyday occurrences but special manifestations for specific redemptive purposes. Paul, who performed extraordinary miracles, also had companions who remained sick (2 Timothy 4:20). Miracles serve as signs pointing to greater realities, not entitlements we can demand. They often cluster around strategic moments of kingdom advancement, spiritual opposition, or specific divine purposes. The gift of miracles operates not according to our expectations but according to God's sovereign wisdom in accomplishing His purposes through supernatural demonstrations at His initiative.

MYTH #3: *"You need perfect faith or holiness to see miracles."*

TRUTH: While both faith and holiness matter deeply, miracles ultimately flow from God's grace rather than human perfection. The disciples performed miracles despite their documented weaknesses and failures. God works through imperfect vessels to demonstrate His power, not ours. Some of the most dramatic miracles occur in settings where human resources, knowledge, and faith seem inadequate—precisely to highlight that the power comes from God, not us. Focus less on achieving some mythical standard of worthiness and more on simple, childlike availability to be used however God chooses.

DISCERNMENT

MYTH #1: *"Discernment is primarily about detecting demonic activity."*
TRUTH: While discerning demonic influence is one aspect of this gift, genuine discernment involves distinguishing between divine, human, and demonic sources. Those with this gift can often recognize when something is flowing from God's Spirit, from human wisdom or emotion, or from dark spiritual influence. Sometimes the greatest danger isn't obvious demonic activity but a subtle mixture—partial truth interwoven with error, genuine giftedness operating from wrong motives, or religious practices disconnected from a relationship with Christ. Mature discernment isn't obsessed with finding demons but with promoting spiritual authenticity and integrity.

MYTH #2: *"Discernment makes you naturally suspicious and critical."*
TRUTH: Healthy discernment isn't rooted in suspicion but in love for truth and concern for spiritual wellbeing. It seeks to protect, not condemn. Those who use this gift judgmentally or with critical spirits are operating from their flesh, not the Spirit's gift. Genuine discernment carries both clarity about falsehood and compassion for those affected by it. Jesus combined perfect discernment with perfect love—He could name deception without demonizing the deceived. The gift

should make you more like Jesus in both truth and grace, not turn you into a spiritual conspiracy theorist.

MYTH #3: *"If two people with discernment disagree, one must be wrong."*

TRUTH: Discernment often reveals different dimensions of complex spiritual realities rather than contradicting valid insights. One person might discern demonic influence, while another discerns the emotional wounds that created vulnerability to it. One might discern false teaching, while another discerns the legitimate spiritual hunger being inappropriately met through that teaching. Instead of dismissing differing discernment, mature practitioners compare insights to develop a more complete understanding. The goal isn't to win discernment contests but to collectively see situations more completely through multiple complementary perspectives.

TONGUES

MYTH #1: *"If you haven't spoken in tongues, you're not really filled with the Holy Spirit."*

TRUTH: While tongues often accompany Spirit baptism in Acts, Paul clearly indicates not all Spirit-filled believers receive this specific gift (1 Cor. 12:30). The Holy Spirit distributes gifts "just as He determines" (1 Cor. 12:11), not according to our doctrinal expectations. Many deeply Spirit-filled believers manifest other gifts without tongues, while others receive this particular grace. The fullness of the Spirit isn't measured by any single manifestation but by the fruit of Christ-like character and the effective operation of whatever gifts He has distributed to each believer for the common good.

MYTH #2: *"Tongues is just emotional gibberish with no real spiritual significance."*

TRUTH: Scripture describes tongues as genuine languages—sometimes known human languages (Acts 2) and sometimes "tongues of angels" (1 Cor. 13:1) unknown to human linguistics. Paul, an intellectual giant, valued this gift highly in his personal devotion, stating "I thank God that I speak in tongues more than all of you" (1 Cor. 14:18). He described specific benefits: edifying oneself (1 Cor. 14:4), praying with one's spirit beyond cognitive limitations (1 Cor. 14:14), and expressing what words cannot capture. This isn't meaningless emotional expression but genuine Spirit-empowered communication that transcends natural language.

MYTH #3: *"Tongues is primarily for public use in church gatherings."*

TRUTH: While public tongues with interpretation have their place, Scripture emphasizes private devotional use more consistently. Paul spent far more time in 1 Corinthians 14 regulating public tongues than promoting them, while affirming their value in personal prayer. Many believers with this gift never exercise it publicly but find it invaluable in private worship, intercession beyond knowledge, and spiritual warfare. Don't measure your gift's legitimacy by public expression—the most significant impact of tongues often happens in personal communion with God, where your spirit prays beyond your mind's limitations.

INTERPRETATION

MYTH #1: *"Interpretation is always a word-for-word translation of tongues."*

TRUTH: While interpretation conveys the essence of what was spoken in tongues, it rarely functions as a literal translation. The Greek word διερμηνεύω (diermēneuō) suggests explaining or expounding meaning rather than strict linguistic conversion. Those with this gift often receive the heart or substance of the message rather than exact words. This explains why interpretations sometimes seem longer or shorter than the tongues' message—the focus is on the faithful communication of the message's meaning and purpose, not on technical linguistic equivalence. The gift operates more like an inspired summary than a verbatim translation.

MYTH #2: *"Anyone who speaks in tongues should automatically be able to interpret."*

TRUTH: While Paul encourages those who speak in tongues to pray for interpretation (1 Cor. 14:13), he clearly distinguishes these as separate gifts distributed by the Spirit's sovereign choice (1 Cor. 12:10). Some believers regularly operate in both gifts, others primarily in one or the other, and many with the tongues gift never receive interpretation. This doesn't invalidate either gift but reflects the Spirit's design for interdependence within the body

11

STRIVING IN YOUR LANE: WHERE YOUR GIFTS MEET THE WORLD'S NEEDS

I remember watching Olympic swimmers during their races—each athlete staying perfectly within their lane, focused entirely on their unique path through the water. There was no wasted energy wondering if they should be swimming someone else's race or questioning whether they belonged in a different lane. They simply poured every ounce of their trained strength into the very space designed for them.

That's what happens when you discover not just your spiritual gifts, but where and how God designed those gifts to operate. There's a holy convergence—a sweet spot where your divine wiring meets specific contexts and needs, precisely as God intended.

The problem is, too many believers have identified their gifts but remain confused about their lane. They're like world-class backstroke swimmers trying to compete in freestyle events—gifted, but misaligned. Or worse, they're standing on the pool deck, watching others swim, wondering if there's a place for them at all.

- *"I know I have the gift of teaching, but I'm not a pastor or professor. Where do I fit?"*

- *"I've got prophetic insight, but I'm a stay-at-home parent. How does that work?"*
- *"My mercy gift seems out of place in my corporate job. Should I just compartmentalize it for church settings?"*

These questions reveal the desperate need for what this chapter offers: practical guidance for finding your lane—the specific contexts and applications where your gifts will create maximum kingdom impact.

Because here's the beautiful truth: God didn't randomly sprinkle gifts across His church. He strategically placed specific gifts in specific people for specific purposes in specific settings. Nothing about your gifting is accidental! Your teaching gift wasn't given just for church classrooms but perhaps for the corporate trainings you develop. Your discernment wasn't meant only for prayer meetings but also for family therapy practice, where you help people identify root issues.

In the pages ahead, we'll explore the diverse lanes where each gift can thrive—from boardrooms to living rooms, from hospitals to highways, from your kitchen table to the marketplace. We'll look at how your gifts might express themselves differently based on your season of life, personality, additional gifts, and divine assignments.

My prayer is that by the end of this chapter, you'll not only know what you're carrying but where it's meant to be delivered. You'll recognize the lanes where your gifting swims most naturally, creating momentum rather than resistance. And you'll see that God's purpose for your gifts extends far beyond church activities into every domain where human lives can be touched by divine love.

So let's discover not just what you're gifted to do, but where you're gifted to do it. It's time to find your lane and swim with everything you've got.

PROPHECY

Your prophetic gift isn't confined to church walls or spiritual settings—it's a divine lens through which you see the world with unusual clarity. You're built to speak truth that cuts through confusion in every arena of life.

Consider how your gift might thrive in:

- **Business environments:** Spotting market trends others miss or identifying the core values a company should build upon
- **Education:** Helping students see beyond surface learning to the deeper principles that will guide their lives
- **Parenting:** Speaking identity and purpose into your children with words that shape their futures
- **Healthcare:** Discerning root causes behind symptoms that others treat superficially
- **Community development:** Articulating a compelling vision of what could be rather than what currently is
- **Creative industries:** Capturing timeless truth in fresh expressions connects with culture
- **Counseling or coaching:** Helping people see their situations from heaven's perspective

SERVING

Your serving gift equips you to see practical needs and meet them with remarkable efficiency and joy. This supernatural ability to remove obstacles and create functional systems makes you invaluable in literally every sphere of human activity.

Consider how your gift might thrive in:

- **Project management:** Your attention to detail ensures nothing falls through the cracks
- **Healthcare:** Anticipating patient needs before they express them
- **Parenting or grandparenting:** Creating environments where family members flourish
- **Entrepreneurship:** Your ability to handle operational details frees others to focus on vision
- **Hospitality industry:** Creating experiences where guests feel genuinely cared for
- **Crisis response:** Whether natural disasters or personal emergencies, you shine when practical needs are urgent
- **Executive support:** Handling logistics enables leaders to function at their best

Don't think for a minute that your gift is somehow less spiritual because it's practical. Jesus Himself said He came "not to be served but to serve" (Mark 10:45). When you coordinate the neighborhood meal train for a family facing cancer, you're not just delivering food; you're delivering tangible grace. When you quietly update your company's inefficient systems, saving everyone hours of frustration, you're not just improving workflow; you're creating space for human flourishing. Your serving gift might look ordinary to casual observers, but it's actually supernatural efficiency empowered by divine love.

TEACHING

Your teaching gift equips you to make complex ideas accessible and applicable. Beyond Sunday School or Bible studies, this gift enables you to help people grasp truth and implement it across every domain of human experience.

Consider how your gift might thrive in:

- **Corporate training:** Your ability to break down complex processes helps teams excel
- **Parenting:** Helping your children understand not just rules, but the principles behind them
- **YouTube or podcasting:** Creating content that makes specialized knowledge accessible
- **Coaching** (athletic, executive, or life): Translating concepts into practical skills
- **Healthcare education:** Helping patients understand treatment plans with clarity
- **Financial advising:** Making complex strategies understandable for clients
- **Skilled trades:** Apprenticeship requires both demonstration and explanation

I know an auto mechanic with the teaching gift who's built a massive YouTube following simply by explaining car repairs with unusual clarity. "I'm not just fixing cars," he told me, "I'm empowering people with understanding." His inbox is filled with messages from viewers who apply his teaching approach to completely different fields.

Your gift isn't just about transferring information; it's about illumination that leads to transformation. When that mental "lightbulb moment" happens for someone because of your explanation, you're witnessing your teaching gift in action. Don't reserve this gift only for overtly spiritual contexts—every domain needs people who can make truth clear and actionable.

GIVING

Your giving gift equips you with supernatural joy and strategic insight for deploying resources for maximum impact. This goes far beyond church offerings; it's about a mindset that sees all resources (money, time, possessions, connections) as tools for blessing others.

Consider how your gift might thrive in:

- **Entrepreneurship:** Creating businesses that generate jobs and opportunities
- **Mentoring:** Investing your experience and wisdom in younger colleagues
- **Real estate:** Developing properties that meet community needs
- **Philanthropy:** Strategically supporting causes with both passion and discernment
- **Investing:** Growing resources specifically to increase your giving capacity
- **Networking:** Connecting people with opportunities or resources they need
- **Community development:** Addressing systemic needs in practical ways

One of the most gifted givers I know runs a modest landscaping business. Nothing about his lifestyle suggests wealth, yet he's helped dozens of young people through college, funded wells in water-scarce regions, and quietly covers medical bills for struggling families. "God doesn't give me resources to increase my standard of living," he says, "but to increase my standard of giving."

Your giving gift might express itself differently from others. You might be drawn to meet immediate needs as they arise, or you might focus on long-term systemic change. You might give anonymously or use your giving to inspire others to join you. However it expresses itself, remember that this gift isn't dependent on wealth; it's about supernatural discernment in stewarding whatever resources God has entrusted to you, whether modest or abundant.

ENCOURAGEMENT

Your encouragement gift equips you to infuse others with courage, hope, and strength when they need it most. This isn't just about saying nice things; it's about a supernatural ability to empower people to take their next step when they might otherwise give up.

Consider how your gift might thrive in:

- **Sales:** Naturally highlighting potential and possibility
- **Human resources:** Helping employees navigate challenges and transitions
- **Physical therapy or rehabilitation:** Progress requires consistent motivation
- **Teaching,** especially with students who doubt their own capabilities
- **Management:** Bringing out the best in team members through strategic affirmation
- **Customer service:** Turning frustrated interactions into positive experiences
- **Crisis intervention:** Providing stability and hope during life's darkest moments

I know a construction foreman with this gift who consistently gets assigned the most challenging crews. "They're not difficult workers," he explains, "they're discouraged workers." His supernatural ability to see potential beneath rough exteriors has salvaged countless careers and lives. "I'm just a guy who hangs drywall," he once told me, "but God uses me to hang hope in people's hearts."

Your encouragement gift might express itself through written notes, timely phone calls, thoughtful gifts, quality time, or words of affirmation, but the impact is the same: people walk away from encounters with you feeling more capable, valued, and hopeful than before. Don't underestimate this gift's power in our discouragement-saturated world. When you encourage authentically, you're not just being nice; you're imparting spiritual strength that can literally change someone's trajectory.

LEADERSHIP

Your leadership gift equips you with a supernatural ability to cast vision and mobilize others toward meaningful objectives. This extends far beyond church committees or ministry teams—it's about catalyzing collective action toward worthwhile goals in any domain.

Consider how your gift might thrive in:

- **Community organizing:** Rallying neighbors around common concerns
- **Entrepreneurship:** Building teams aligned around a compelling vision
- **Family life:** Creating a healthy culture and direction in your home

- **Project management:** Keeping diverse stakeholders moving toward shared objectives
- **Sports coaching:** Developing both individual talent and team cohesion
- **Political engagement:** Advocating for policies that serve the common good
- **Volunteer coordination:** Maximizing impact through strategic deployment

Your leadership gift might be expressed through different styles—you might be visionary or methodical, relational or analytical, bold or understated. The expression varies, but the essence remains: You help people move from where they are to where they should be. True leadership isn't about position or authority; it's about serving others by showing them what's possible and helping them get there together. When you lead from this mindset—whether in boardrooms, community meetings, or family dinner tables—you're exercising your gift as God intended.

MERCY

Your mercy gift equips you with supernatural compassion and the capacity to enter others' pain without being destroyed by it. This goes far beyond church benevolence committees—it's about bringing God's tender care into the broken places of human experience wherever you encounter them.

Consider how your gift might thrive in:

- **Healthcare:** Clinical skill paired with compassion creates true healing

- **Justice system:** Bringing restorative approaches to broken situations
- **Customer service,** especially in settings dealing with people in distress
- **Crisis response:** Providing emotional support during disasters or emergencies
- **Hospice care:** Walking with families through end-of-life journeys
- **Special education:** Creating dignifying experiences for those with differences
- **Conflict resolution:** Helping restore relationships in families, workplaces, or communities

I know a mechanic with this gift who's built his business around serving single moms and elderly customers who are often exploited elsewhere. "I'm not just fixing cars," he says. "I'm providing peace of mind to people who feel vulnerable." His waiting room often resembles a counseling office more than an auto shop as customers share their struggles with someone they trust won't judge them.

Your mercy gift might be expressed through practical help, emotional presence, or advocacy for the overlooked, but the impact is the same: People who society often deems "problems to solve" instead experience being valued as people to love. In our efficiency-obsessed culture, your countercultural willingness to slow down and truly see suffering creates space for genuine healing. Don't reserve this gift only for dramatic situations—sometimes mercy's greatest impact comes through small moments of dignity offered consistently over time.

APOSTLE

Your apostolic gift equips you with supernatural vision to pioneer new territory and establish foundations others can build upon. This extends far beyond church planting—it's about entrepreneurial breakthrough in any domain that advances kingdom values in fresh ways.

Consider how your gift might thrive in:

- **Business startups,** especially those addressing unmet needs or underserved markets
- **Education innovation:** Developing new approaches to learning challenges
- **Cross-cultural work,** whether international or across social divides
- **Organizational development:** Creating systems that can scale and replicate
- **Industry disruption:** Challenging status quo approaches with better alternatives
- **Community transformation:** Addressing systemic issues with comprehensive approaches
- **Mentoring networks:** Developing leaders who will multiply your impact

I met a woman with apostolic gifting who noticed the lack of holistic support for single mothers in her city. Rather than simply starting another program, she pioneered an integrated approach connecting housing, childcare, education, and employment opportunities through a network of existing organizations. "I'm not building my own empire," she explains. "I'm creating infrastructure that empowers others to be more effective together than they could be separately."

Your apostolic gift might manifest through launching new initiatives, reimagining existing systems, or building bridges between disconnected domains. You're energized by challenge, undaunted by opposition, and driven by a vision of what could be rather than what currently is. While others maintain existing structures (an essential role!), you're built to push beyond boundaries into uncharted territory. Whether establishing new businesses, developing creative approaches to old problems, or forming cross-cultural connections, your willingness to go first creates pathways that others can later travel more easily.

EVANGELIST

Your evangelistic gift equips you with a supernatural ability to communicate persuasively and help people embrace new perspectives. While this certainly applies to sharing faith, the essence of this gift—helping people cross thresholds toward positive change—applies across countless domains.

Consider how your gift might thrive in:

- **Sales:** Helping people see value and overcome objections
- **Change management** within organizations navigating transitions
- **Healthcare education:** Motivating lifestyle modifications for better outcomes
- **Environmental advocacy:** Inspiring practical steps toward sustainability
- **Marketing:** Crafting messages that genuinely resonate and motivate
- **Addiction recovery:** Helping people envision and embrace transformation

- **Recruitment:** Attracting talent by effectively communicating vision and culture

I know a real estate agent with this gift who sees his role as far more than selling properties. "I'm helping people transition to new chapters in their stories," he says. His supernatural ability to understand what truly matters to clients, address their fears, and paint a compelling picture of possibility makes him exceptionally effective, not because he's manipulative, but because he genuinely believes in the positive impact of right decisions.

Your evangelistic gift might be expressed through public speaking, one-on-one conversation, written communication, or creative media, but the impact is consistent: People who were hesitant or resistant become open and receptive. You naturally build bridges between where people are and where they could be. This gift isn't about forced persuasion but about an authentic invitation that respects others' freedom while clearly presenting the benefits of change. Whether you're literally sharing the gospel or helping people embrace other positive transitions, your gift creates momentum toward better futures.

SHEPHERD

Your shepherding gift equips you with a supernatural capacity to nurture growth and development in others through attentive care over time. This extends far beyond church pastoring; it's about creating a safe space for authentic development in any context where relationships matter.

Consider how your gift might thrive in:

- **Management:** Developing team members through personalized care and guidance

- **Education:** Nurturing both academic growth and character development
- **Healthcare,** especially in ongoing care relationships like primary medicine or therapy
- **Mentoring:** Providing consistent guidance through life and career transitions
- **Hospitality industry:** Creating experiences where guests feel genuinely seen and valued
- **Parenting or grandparenting:** Nurturing the unique potential in each child
- **Community building:** Fostering authentic connection in neighborhoods or organizations

Your shepherding gift might express through one-on-one relationships, small group facilitation, or organizational leadership, but the essence remains consistent: You create environments where people feel safe enough to be authentic and supported enough to grow. Unlike those who focus primarily on tasks or goals, you naturally prioritize the people themselves. This isn't inefficient sentimentality; it's strategic investment in sustainable development. Whether in companies, classrooms, or communities, your gift creates cultures where genuine flourishing happens from the inside out.

WISDOM

Your wisdom gift equips you with supernatural insight that cuts through complexity to identify core issues and viable solutions. This extends far beyond church counsel; it's about bringing heaven's perspective to bear on earthly challenges in any domain where discernment matters.

Consider how your gift might thrive in:

- **Organizational leadership,** especially in navigating complex decisions or conflicts
- **Counseling or coaching:** Helping others see situations from new perspectives
- **Mediation:** Identifying common ground in seemingly opposed positions
- **Strategic planning:** Discerning which opportunities align with deeper purposes
- **Parenting,** especially through challenging developmental stages or circumstances
- **Financial advising:** Seeing beyond numbers to underlying values and priorities
- **Community leadership:** Addressing systemic issues with a nuanced understanding

Your wisdom gift might express through thoughtful counsel, incisive questions, strategic suggestions, or reframing perspectives, but the impact is consistent: Complexity becomes navigable, and seemingly impossible situations reveal hidden possibilities. Unlike mere knowledge or intelligence, wisdom involves discernment that transcends normal understanding. This isn't about having all the answers; it's about asking the right questions and seeing connections others miss. Whether in corporate boardrooms, community meetings, or kitchen table conversations, your gift creates clarity where confusion once prevailed.

SPECIAL KNOWLEDGE

Your knowledge gift equips you with supernatural access to specific information that couldn't be known through natural means. This extends beyond church settings; it's about receiving divine insight in any context where hidden understanding can unlock a breakthrough.

Consider how your gift might thrive in:

- **Investigative work,** whether journalism, research, or problem-solving
- **Medical diagnosis:** Perceiving conditions that standard tests miss
- **Business strategy:** Receiving unexpected insight into market trends or opportunities
- **Counseling or therapy:** Discerning root issues beneath presenting symptoms
- **Mechanical or technical troubleshooting:** Identifying problems others overlook
- **Parenting:** Understanding what your child isn't saying but needs you to know
- **Crisis intervention:** Quickly assessing situations with unusual accuracy

I know a teacher with this gift who regularly receives specific insights about her students' home situations without being told. "I'm not just teaching curriculum," she says. "I'm seeing beyond behavior to the stories driving it." Her supernatural perception allows her to address real needs rather than just symptoms, creating breakthroughs where traditional approaches would fail.

Your knowledge gift might come through sudden impressions, mental pictures, dreams, physical sensations, or simply "knowing" without explanation, but the result is consistent: hidden information becomes available precisely when needed. This isn't about being psychic or omniscient; it's about receiving targeted divine insight for specific redemptive purposes.

Whether in boardrooms, classrooms, or living rooms, your gift unveils what's hidden beneath the surface, creating opportunities for healing, growth, and breakthrough where others see only dead ends.

FAITH

Your faith gift equips you with supernatural confidence that stands firm when circumstances, emotions, and even logic suggest surrender. This extends far beyond church prayer meetings; it's about maintaining divine certainty in any context where human impossibility meets God's promises.

Consider how your gift might thrive in:

- **Entrepreneurship,** especially pioneering ventures that others deem impossible
- **Crisis leadership:** Providing stability when everything seems to be collapsing
- **Special needs parenting:** Maintaining vision and hope through relentless challenges
- **Organizational turnarounds:** Believing in renewal when decline seems inevitable
- **Medical challenges:** Maintaining supernatural confidence amid discouraging diagnoses
- **Social reform:** Persistently addressing entrenched problems despite slow progress
- **Disaster recovery:** Rebuilding when devastation makes restoration seem impossible

I watched a documentary about a school principal with this gift who took over a failing school that everyone had written off. "I'm not just managing an institution," she explains.

"I'm standing in the gap between what is and what could be." Her supernatural certainty that transformation was possible—despite overwhelming evidence to the contrary—created space for a miraculous turnaround that statistics couldn't predict.

Your faith gift might express through calm confidence, bold declarations, persistent prayers, or visionary planning in the face of apparent impossibility, but the impact is consistent: what others abandon as hopeless, you continue to believe in until breakthrough comes. This isn't blind optimism or wishful thinking; it's a divine impartation of certainty that transcends circumstances. Whether in hospitals, startups, or community initiatives, your gift creates momentum when everyone else has lost hope and perseverance when giving up seems the only rational option.

HEALING

Your healing gift equips you with a supernatural capacity to be a channel for God's restorative power. This extends beyond physical ailments and church healing lines; it's about facilitating wholeness in any context where brokenness diminishes human flourishing.

Consider how your gift might thrive in:

- **Healthcare,** where clinical skill combines with supernatural compassion
- **Reconciliation work:** Healing divisions in families, communities, or organizations
- **Environmental restoration:** Bringing healing to damaged ecosystems
- **Trauma recovery:** Creating a safe space for deep emotional healing

- **Addiction services:** Facilitating freedom from destructive patterns
- **Organizational healing:** Restoring trust and function after crisis or conflict
- **Arts therapy:** Using creative expression to facilitate healing in non-verbal ways

Your healing gift might express through prayer, touch, words, presence, creative arts, or practical service, but the outcome is consistent: Restoration begins where brokenness once seemed permanent. This gift isn't just about dramatic instantaneous miracles (though these certainly occur); it's often about facilitating processes of restoration that unfold over time. Whether in hospitals, broken relationships, or damaged communities, your gift creates pathways toward wholeness where division, disease, or dysfunction once prevailed.

MIRACLES

Your miracles gift equips you with supernatural authority to see God intervene in ways that defy natural explanation. This extends beyond church services; it's about participating in divine disruption of natural patterns in any context where human capacity reaches its limit.

Consider how your gift might thrive in:

- **Crisis intervention,** when normal solutions can't address the urgency
- **Resource limitations:** Seeing supernatural provision where natural supply is exhausted
- **"Impossible" turnarounds** in businesses, relationships, or health situations

- **Natural disasters,** where supernatural protection or provision becomes essential
- **Systemic challenges** that have resisted conventional approaches
- **Deadline impossibilities,** when natural time constraints make completion unfeasible
- **Specialized problem-solving,** where conventional wisdom has no answers

Your miracles gift might manifest through dramatic interventions, supernatural coincidences, inexplicable provisions, or divine protection, but the impact is consistent: What was naturally impossible becomes reality. This gift isn't about creating spectacles or drawing attention to yourself; it's about partnering with God in situations where human capacity has reached its limit. Whether in dire medical scenarios, desperate financial circumstances, or seemingly hopeless family situations, your gift creates a breakthrough precisely when human wisdom says, "There's nothing more we can do."

DISCERNMENT

Your discernment gift equips you with supernatural ability to distinguish between divine, human, and deceptive spiritual influences. This extends far beyond church contexts; it's about accurately perceiving underlying realities in any situation where discerning truth from counterfeit is at stake.

Consider how your gift might thrive in:

- **Business negotiations:** Sensing hidden agendas or authentic opportunities

- **Hiring processes:** Perceiving character beyond resume qualifications
- **Mentoring relationships:** Identifying authentic potential versus self-deception
- **Media evaluation:** Distinguishing truth from manipulation in information sources
- **Investment decisions:** Sensing sustainable value versus attractive facades
- **Relationship counseling:** Identifying root issues beneath presenting problems
- **Team building:** Creating authentic cultures that resist toxic influences

I know another real estate agent with this gift who consistently steers clients away from properties that later reveal serious hidden problems. "I'm not just selling houses," she explains. "I'm protecting people's largest investment and family sanctuary." Her supernatural ability to sense when something is "off"—despite no visible evidence—has saved countless clients from disastrous purchases that would have passed standard inspections.

Your discernment gift might express through gut feelings, mental clarity, physical reactions, or spiritual impressions, but the outcome is consistent: What remains hidden to others becomes visible to you. This isn't about being judgmental or suspicious; it's about perceiving reality accurately so you can respond appropriately. Whether in boardrooms, family decisions, or community partnerships, your gift creates protection from deception and guidance toward authentic paths when multiple options all appear legitimate on the surface.

TONGUES

Your tongues gift equips you with supernatural communication that transcends natural language limitations. While distinctly spiritual in nature, this gift impacts far more than church services; it's about accessing deeper communion and expression in any context where natural language falls short. Consider how your gift might thrive in:

- **Intercession,** for situations too complex for cognitive understanding
- **Cross-cultural work:** Building spiritual bridges across language barriers
- **Worship leadership:** Facilitating deeper spiritual experience
- **Spiritual warfare:** Addressing opposition beyond intellectual comprehension
- **Creative blocks:** Breaking through limitations in artistic expression
- **Personal devotion:** Deepening intimate communion with God
- **Decision crossroads:** Seeking guidance beyond rational analysis

Your tongues gift might express through known languages you've never learned, heavenly languages unknown to human linguistics, or forms of expression beyond verbal communication, but the impact is consistent: Limitations of natural language are transcended. This isn't about spiritual performance or public display; it's about accessing communion and communication beyond cognitive constraints. Whether in private devotion, challenging intercession, or appropriate public settings with interpretation, your gift creates pathways for divine communication when human language proves inadequate for the depth required.

INTERPRETATION

Your interpretation gift equips you with a supernatural understanding of spiritual communications that would otherwise remain mysterious. This extends beyond church tongues messages; it's about bringing clarity to any context where divine meaning needs to be translated into human understanding.

Consider how your gift might thrive in:

- **Cross-cultural communication:** Bridging language and cultural gaps
- **Conflict resolution:** Translating between perspectives that seem irreconcilable
- **Dream interpretation:** Discerning symbolic meaning in dreams or visions
- **Translation work:** Capturing essence beyond literal meaning
- **Teaching complex topics:** Making difficult concepts accessible
- **Artistic interpretation:** Helping others connect with deeper meaning in creative work
- **Spiritual guidance:** Helping others understand what God might be saying to them

Your interpretation gift might be expressed through spontaneous understanding of unknown languages, insight into symbolic communication, or the ability to translate complex spiritual concepts into accessible terms, but the outcome is consistent: What was mysterious becomes meaningful. This isn't about impressive spiritual performance; it's about building bridges between divine communication and human comprehension. Whether interpreting tongues, messages, dreams, or complex spiritual impressions, your gift creates clarity where confusion once prevented understanding and application.

12

THE GIFTED MIRROR TEST[IP]

> *Do not merely listen to the word, and so deceive yourselves. Do what it says. Anyone who listens to the word but does not do what it says is like someone who looks at his face in a mirror and, after looking at himself, goes away and immediately forgets what he looks like. But whoever looks intently into the perfect law that gives freedom, and continues in it—not forgetting what they have heard, but doing it—they will be blessed in what they do.*
>
> —James 1:22–25

By now, you've likely taken assessments, read profiles, and identified patterns that confirm what the Holy Spirit has been whispering to your heart for years: You are gifted. Not randomly. Not accidentally. But intentionally, strategically, divinely gifted for a purpose that only you can fulfill.

But here's where things get dangerous.

James warns us about something that happens to well-meaning people every single day—people just like you and me. They encounter the truth that could transform their lives; they nod in agreement, feel inspired for a moment... and then walk away unchanged. They become what James calls "forgetful hearers."

I've watched it happen countless times. Someone discovers they have the gift of encouragement and gets excited about it for about two weeks. Then life gets busy, circumstances get complicated, and the revelation gets filed away with all the other "good ideas" they'll get to someday. A year later, when someone asks about their spiritual gifts, they can barely remember what they scored on their assessment.

That's not going to be you. Not if I have anything to say about it.

THE MIRROR MOMENT

James uses this powerful image of someone looking in a mirror. Picture yourself right now, holding up the Scripture in this book like a mirror to your soul. What have you seen? What has God revealed about the supernatural capacity He's placed within you?

Maybe you've recognized yourself in the mercy profiles and finally understand why broken people are drawn to you like magnets. Perhaps you've discovered that your natural ability to see solutions isn't just intelligence; it's the gift of wisdom breaking through. Or you've realized that your compulsion to speak truth isn't just stubbornness; it's a prophetic gift that this world desperately needs.

Whatever you've seen in this mirror, James is crystal clear about what happens next. You have two choices:

Choice 1: Walk away and forget. Go back to thinking your gifts are just personality quirks or natural abilities. Resume life as usual, complaining about the lack of purpose and meaning while ignoring the supernatural equipment God has given you to create exactly the life you're longing for.

Choice 2: Look intently, continue in it, and do what you've learned. Let this revelation mark the turning point where you stop living beneath your spiritual capacity and start unleashing what God has placed within you.

The difference between these two choices isn't just what you know; ***it's what you do with what you know.***

FROM HEARING TO DOING

Remember Gideon? When the angel called him a "mighty hero" while he was hiding in a winepress, he could have dismissed it as wishful thinking. Instead, he took the step he could take with the strength he had. That single step of obedience transformed a fearful farmer into the deliverer of Israel.

That's the power of moving from hearing to doing.

Throughout this book, we've dismantled the myths that keep gifts dormant. We've identified the lanes where your gifts can thrive. We've seen how your gifts aren't just for church settings but for every domain of your life: your workplace, your family, your community, your calling.

But all of that discovery means nothing if you don't take action.

THE DECEPTION OF SPIRITUAL KNOWLEDGE

James uses a shocking word here. He says that if we hear but don't do, we "deceive ourselves." Not that we're deceived by someone else, but that we become our own deceivers.

How does this self-deception work? It's actually quite simple and tragically common.

We convince ourselves that knowing equals doing. We think that because we can identify our gifts, we're automatically walking in them. We assume that because we understand biblical principles about giftedness, we're living them out.

We mistake spiritual information for spiritual transformation.

But here's the hard truth: Satan isn't concerned with how much you know about your gifts as long as you don't actually use them. He's perfectly fine with you having clear theology about spiritual gifts, taking assessments, reading books, and even teaching others—as long as your own gifts remain theoretical rather than operational.

> **WE MISTAKE SPIRITUAL INFORMATION FOR SPIRITUAL TRANSFORMATION.**

The most spiritually informed generation in history is often the most spiritually ineffective. Why? Because we've confused education with activation, information with transformation, and hearing with doing.

WHAT DOES "DOING" LOOK LIKE?

So what does it mean to "do" what you've learned about your gifts?

It means the woman who discovered her prophetic gift stops editing herself and starts speaking the truth God gives her with love and courage. It means the man with mercy gifts sets healthy boundaries so he can serve from a place of strength rather than exhaustion. It means the teacher finds ways to explain complex concepts at work, not just in Bible studies.

"Doing" means taking the step that's right in front of you.

Maybe that's offering to pray for healing when someone mentions they're sick. Maybe it's volunteering to coordinate event logistics because you have serving gifts. Maybe it's asking thoughtful questions that help someone process their situation because you carry the gift of wisdom.

It's less dramatic than you think and more powerful than you can imagine.

I know a businessman who discovered his gift of encouragement. Instead of waiting for some grand ministry opportunity, he started sending one text message each morning to someone who needed encouragement. Five years later, he has a contact list of hundreds of people who've given him permission to speak into their lives regularly. What started as simple obedience has become a widespread ministry that's impacted countless lives.

That's what "doing" produces: supernatural multiplication of natural faithfulness.

THE FREEDOM PROMISE

But here's the beautiful part of James' teaching that we can't miss. He says that those who look intently into God's truth and continue in it will be "blessed in what they do."

The word "blessed" here isn't about receiving external rewards. It's about experiencing the **deep satisfaction, purpose, and freedom** that come from living aligned with God's design for your life.

When you walk in your gifts, you experience what Jesus called "life to the full." Not because life becomes easier, but because you're finally living as the person God created you to be.

You know that feeling when you're operating in your gifts? When time seems to disappear because you're so engaged in what you're doing? When people comment, "You're so good at that!" and you think, "This doesn't even feel like work"? When you see the impact your gift creates and think, "I can't believe God gets to use me like this"?

That's the freedom James is talking about. That's the blessing of doing, not just hearing.

THE URGENCY OF NOW

I need to tell you something with all the pastoral love I can muster: You don't have forever to figure this out.

I don't mean that to scare you, but to awaken you to the reality that your gifts aren't just for you; they're for the people around you who need what God has placed within you.

Right now. Today.

There's someone in your orbit who needs your mercy gift to help them heal from trauma they can't process alone.

> THE WORLD DOESN'T NEED YOU TO BECOME SOMEONE DIFFERENT. IT NEEDS YOU TO BECOME FULLY WHO GOD MADE YOU TO BE.

There's a situation in your workplace that requires your discernment to navigate safely. There's a conversation waiting to happen where your words of knowledge could unlock a breakthrough someone has been praying for.

Every day you postpone walking in your gifts is another day that impact remains unmade, healing remains unavailable, truth remains unspoken, encouragement remains undelivered.

The world doesn't need you to become someone different. It needs you to become fully who God made you to be.

YOUR MIRROR TEST

So here's my challenge to you—your mirror test, if you will.

Look in the mirror of your soul one more time and ask yourself: "What is God calling me to do with what I now know about how He's gifted me?"

Don't overthink it. Don't wait for the perfect opportunity or the ideal circumstances. Don't postpone action until you feel more qualified or less afraid.

Just answer this question: Based on what you've learned about your gifts, what's one specific step you can take this week?

Maybe it's having a conversation you've been avoiding because you know your prophetic gift needs to speak truth in love. Maybe it's volunteering for something that perfectly aligns with your serving gift. Maybe it's offering to pray for someone because your healing gift is stirring.

Whatever it is, the time to do it is now.

Because the difference between a life of purpose and a life of regret isn't usually dramatic. It's simply the accumulated impact of taking the next right step when God reveals it.

THE CHOICE IS YOURS

James ends his teaching with a choice that each of us must make: Will we be hearers only, or will we be doers?

Will we let the ideas in this book join the pile of good ideas that never became lived realities? Or will we let it mark the moment when we stopped living beneath our capacity and started unleashing the power within?

You've been given everything you need. God has placed supernatural gifts within you. The Holy Spirit stands ready to empower their expression. The body of Christ needs what you carry. The world is waiting for the love of Jesus to be demonstrated through your unique giftedness.

The only question remaining is: What will you do?

Remember, you were gifted ON purpose FOR purpose. Not to impress people with your abilities, but to demonstrate God's love through your availability. Not to build your own kingdom, but to advance His. Not to find your worth in your performance, but to find your joy in your obedience.

When you step into your gifts—when you move from hearing to doing—you'll discover what countless believers before you have discovered: There's nothing quite like the satisfaction of being used by God for the very purposes you were created to fulfill.

So go ahead. Take the step. Use your gifts. Trust the process. Your purpose is waiting.

Reflection Questions

1. **THE MIRROR MOMENT** Right now, in this moment, what is God's Spirit stirring in you about your spiritual gifts? What specific gift or combination of gifts is He highlighting as your next area for growth and action?

2. **THE BARRIER CHECK** What fear, misconception, or circumstance has been your primary excuse for not fully walking in your gifts? How might God be calling you to move past this barrier?

3. **THE FIRST STEP** What is one specific, concrete action you can take within the next seven days to begin expressing your spiritual gifts more intentionally? (Be specific: Who will you contact? What will you offer to do? Where will you step up?)

4. **THE ACCOUNTABILITY FACTOR** Who is one person you can share your gift discovery with who will help you stay accountable to walking in your calling? When will you have this conversation?

5. **THE VISION CAST** Six months from now, if you were fully walking in your spiritual gifts on purpose FOR purpose, what would be different about your life, your relationships, and your impact on others?

13

WHAT'S NEXT?

> *The man who had received five bags of gold went at once and put his money to work and gained five bags more. So also, the one with two bags of gold gained two more. But the man who had received one bag went off, dug a hole in the ground and hid his master's money.*
>
> —Matthew 25:16–18 NIV

The parable of the steward is one of Jesus' most powerful teachings. Once the servants were entrusted with their "talents," they immediately put them to work, and they grew. The one with five gained five more, and the one with two gained two more. However, there always seems to be that one who did nothing with what they'd been given.

Have you noticed the urgency in Jesus' story? The first two servants didn't attend a seminar on investment strategies or join a committee to discuss potential options. They went "at once" and put their talents to work. There's a holy urgency that accompanies divine giftedness. God has placed supernatural abilities within you for this moment, not for some distant future when everything is perfectly aligned.

I hope this book has *inspired you, cautioned you,* and *encouraged you* to understand that you've been Gifted ON Purpose FOR Purpose. Now it's time to apply that understanding and put it to work immediately. Like all great things God has given us, it requires our participation in order for it to grow. God gives us our faith, but we must exercise it in order to see it grow. The same is true of our giftedness.

Maybe you're more difficult to inspire. Perhaps my challenge has simply not been enough. There's a chance that my writing style doesn't move you the way I hope it will. No matter the case, if you've not reached a tipping point in your mind by now, then let the words of Matthew 25:19 add the final weight.

> *After a long time, their master returned from his trip and called them to give an account of how they had used his money.*
>
> —Matthew 25:19

WE ARE ACCOUNTABLE

No one knows how long their life will be. Like the servants in this parable, they didn't know when the Master would return. So what did they do? They immediately began to put their master's money to work, and "after a long time…" they met with the Master again and were called to give an account of how they had used what He had entrusted to them.

Think about this for a moment: every spiritual gift you've been given comes with a future conversation attached to it. Someday, you and I will sit across from Jesus himself, and He'll ask, "What did you do with what I gave you?" It won't be a general question about your life—it will be specifically about those unique abilities He purposefully placed within you. The gifts you've discovered through this book aren't just nice-to-know information; they're divine deposits that God expects a return on.

I want you to experience the incredible **purpose** that living ON purpose FOR purpose will bring to you and your life! Feel your strength within grow as you lean into the Holy Spirit and trust Him to work through those gifts in every area of your life.

I want you to experience the **transformation** that will come when you begin using your gifts! Watch your gifts grow in strength and reliability like a muscle being worked out. This will not only allow you to grow spiritually but will also transform those you are serving with your gifts.

I want you to experience the **impact** of living out your giftedness on this world! Experience how your gifts are multiplied when they are fueled by the love of Christ and impact the world as you are living on mission for Him.

I want you to experience a full and satisfying life through your Gifts.

But above all else, I want you to experience the celebration that Jesus wants to share with you.

> **TO BE HELD ACCOUNTABLE SHOULD NOT MOTIVATE US BY FEAR, BUT RATHER BY REWARD.**

> *The master was full of praise. 'Well done, my good and faithful servant. You have been faithful in handling this small amount, so now I will give you many more responsibilities. Let's celebrate together!*
>
> —Matthew 25:21

To be held accountable should not motivate us by fear, but rather by reward. Everyone who uses well what God has entrusted to them, not only receives more, but also enjoys the celebration with the Master. The reward is not just the benefits of leveraging our gifts, but also the opportunity to share that reward with the One who entrusted us with those gifts.

I've often wondered what that celebration looks like. Can you imagine Jesus, eyes bright with joy, saying, "Remember that time you stepped out and used your gift of encouragement with that struggling coworker? Let me show you what happened next in their life because of your faithfulness." Or perhaps, "Remember when you used your gift of service during that crisis? Let me introduce you to the people who came to know me because they saw my love through you." This isn't just about avoiding punishment; it's about entering into the pure delight of your Master as He reveals the full impact of your purposeful living.

KEEP THIS BOOK AS A RESOURCE

Over the next several years, you will more than likely experience two things.

First, you will have some incredible experiences with God as you begin to use and live out of your giftedness. That's a guarantee! Whenever you take a step towards God, He always meets you there. There are countless awesome moments ahead for you.

The second experience you will have is one that naturally drifts you back towards your old life. The pull to "take it easy" and "don't be so serious about this gifted stuff" will start immediately, and, combined with the stress and distractions of life, you will drift back to your old ways. This is not negative self-talk; this is simply the reality of our flesh.

When those times come, crack open this book and revisit your favorite chapters. This book was created as a resource to support you throughout your gifted journey. I've prayed that something in this book will be used in years to come to help put you back on track to living the gifted life!

Maybe it's the chapter on purpose that you need a reminder of. Maybe it's just the story of Gideon, where God always sees who He has made you to be, not what you see in your current circumstances. Perhaps it is simply this chapter, reminding you that we're accountable for what we've been entrusted with, and that for those who intentionally live the gifted life, there is a celebration that Jesus is planning to enjoy with you!

Life has a way of clouding our spiritual vision. The urgent demands of daily living can make us forget the important truths we once embraced with passion. That's why spiritual amnesia is one of our enemy's most effective tactics. He doesn't have to make you reject your gifts—he just has to make you forget about them.

Put this book somewhere visible.

Set calendar reminders to revisit your gifting.

Find accountability partners who will ask you regularly how you're stewarding what God has given you.

Never forget: You've been gifted ON purpose FOR purpose. You've been gifted with the experience of transformation through the renewing of your mind. You've been gifted to impact this world with the love of Jesus Christ!

Now it's time to Live ON Purpose FOR Purpose!

Reflection Questions

1. In the parable of the talents, the first two servants acted "at once." What is one immediate step you can take this week to begin using your primary spiritual gift more intentionally? What might be holding you back from taking this step?

2. How does the reality of future accountability to Jesus change your perspective on developing and using your spiritual gifts? Does this motivate you more by the promise of reward or by fear of disappointment?

3. In what area of your life (work, home, community, church) do you feel God is specifically calling you to invest your spiritual gifts right now? Why do you think God has positioned you in this particular place at this particular time?

4. What specific distractions or pressures tend to pull you away from living on purpose FOR purpose? What practical safeguards could you put in place to help you stay focused on your divine calling?

5. Imagine your future conversation with Jesus about how you stewarded your gifts. What would you love to hear Him say about how you used what He entrusted to you? What steps can you take now to make that conversation a celebration rather than a regret?

ENDNOTES

1. "Definition of Spiritual Gifts: Gifts Test," Definition of Spiritual Gifts | Gifts Test, accessed October 6, 2025, http://giftstest.com/allgifts.
2. "Shorter Catechism," Bible Presbyterian Church General Synod, accessed October 6, 2025, http://www.shortercatechism.com/resources/wsc/wsc_001.html.
3. "Mission, Vision, & Values: Journey Church: A Church in Huntersville, NC," Journey Church | A Church in Huntersville, NC, accessed October 6, 2025, http://thejourneyonline.com/about-us/mission-vision/.
4. James Strong, *Strong's Exhaustive Concordance of the Bible* (Nashville, TN: Abingdon, 1981).
5. Matthew Henry and Leslie F. Church, *Matthew Henry's Commentary on the Whole Bible in One Volume: Genesis to Revelation* (London, UK: Marshall, Morgan & Scott, 1973).
6. A. T. Robertson and Wesley J. Perschbacher, *Word Pictures of the New Testament* (Grand Rapids, MI: Kregel Publications, 2004).
7. Strong, *The Exhaustive Concordance of the Bible*.
8. Strong, *The Exhaustive Concordance of the Bible*.
9. Henry and Church, *Commentary on the Whole Bible*.
10. Robertson and Perschbacher, *Word Pictures of the New Testament*.
11. Strong, *The Exhaustive Concordance of the Bible*.

12. Matthew Henry and Leslie F. Church, *Matthew Henry's Commentary on the Whole Bible in One Volume: Genesis to Revelation*
13. A. T. Robertson and Wesley J. Perschbacher, *Word Pictures of the New Testament.*
14. John Rea and Ray Corvin, *The Layman's Commentary on the Holy Spirit* (Plainfield, NJ: Logos International, 1974).
15. Institute in Basic Life Principles, *Understanding Spiritual Gifts*, IBLP Publications, Oak Brook, Illinois, 1986.
16. Strong, *Strong's Exhaustive Concordance of the Bible.*
17. Wayne Grudem, *Systematic Theology: An Introduction to Biblical Doctrine*, Inter-Varsity Press, Leicester, England, and Zondervan Publishing House, Grand Rapids, Michigan, 1994.
18. Strong, *Strong's Exhaustive Concordance of the Bible.*
19. Strong, *Strong's Exhaustive Concordance of the Bible.*
20. Strong, *Strong's Exhaustive Concordance of the Bible.*
21. Henry and Church, *Commentary on the Whole Bible.*
22. Robertson and Perschbacher, *Word Pictures of the New Testament.*
23. Strong, *Strong's Exhaustive Concordance of the Bible.*
24. Strong, *Strong's Exhaustive Concordance of the Bible.*
25. Robertson and Perschbacher, Word Pictures of the New Testament.
26. Strong, *Strong's Exhaustive Concordance of the Bible.*
27. Arnold Bittlinger, *Gifts and Graces: A Commentary on I Corinthians 12-14* (Grand Rapids, MI: Eerdmans, 1976).
28. General Information https://spiritualgiftstest.com

ACKNOWLEDGMENTS

Every book has a moment of conception, and this one began with my wife, Tracie Dawson. While she was pouring her heart into writing *Crowning Wisdom*, she saw something in me I hadn't yet recognized—a message that needed to escape the walls of our local church and find its way onto paper. Tracie, you didn't just encourage me to write; you showed me what it looks like to wrestle words onto a page while life keeps happening all around us. In 2015, while expecting our third child, we were both racing toward our individual finish lines, cheering each other on through exhaustion and excitement. You've been my first reader, my toughest critic, and my fiercest champion through every version of this message. Thank you for believing this book mattered before I even knew it was a book.

Sometimes, God uses a single sermon to redirect your entire trajectory. Over fifteen years ago, I sat in a breakout session in Tulsa, Oklahoma, listening to Willie George teach on spiritual gifts, and everything I thought I knew began to unravel—in the best possible way. Willie, you'll probably never know this, but that session forced me to confront the gap between the church experience I grew up in and what Scripture actually says about spiritual gifts. You started me on a journey that led here.

To Don Gentry and Chris Denning—brothers who served alongside me on our leadership team—thank you for refusing to let me keep this message small. Every time I taught it, you pushed me to make it clearer, more accessible, more practical.

You saw what this could become long before I did, and your encouragement kept me refining when I wanted to settle for "good enough."

The real heroes of this book are the Journey Church family members whose stories fill these pages. You took these teachings and did something beautiful—you actually lived them out. Watching you discover your gifts in your workplaces, marriages, and everyday moments; seeing God show up in ways that surprised even you—those testimonies are what convinced me this message wasn't just true, it was necessary. You turned theology into biography, and your courage to step into your gifting challenged me to keep this book relentlessly practical.

To my children, who've watched their dad disappear into his office countless evenings to "work on the book"—thank you for sharing me with this project. Your encouragement to pursue the longer, harder path of professional publishing, even when I wanted to take shortcuts, reminds me that you're watching and learning what it means to steward a calling.

Dr. Tim Elmore, that writing mastermind in Atlanta, changed everything. You didn't just give me tools; you gave me permission to do the hard work of resurrection—to take something I'd buried in 2015 and breathe new life into it. Thank you for introducing me to Kary Oberbrunner and his incredible team, who saw what this book could become and partnered with me to make it happen.

To the Journey Church staff and congregation who've endured countless sermon series, workshops, and conversations about spiritual gifts—you've been my laboratory, my sounding board, and my greatest encouragement. You've proven that when everyday believers understand they're gifted ON purpose FOR purpose, the supernatural becomes normal.

Finally, to everyone who's ever felt like their gifts don't matter, who's been told to sit down and be quiet, who's wondered if God really has a purpose for them—this book exists because of you and for you. Thank you for the courage to keep searching for what God placed inside you. Your hunger for more inspired every page.

The truth is, no one writes alone. This book carries the fingerprints of a community that believes the Church's best days aren't behind us—they're waiting to be unleashed through believers who finally understand they're carrying supernatural capacity for Kingdom impact.

Let's unleash it together.

ABOUT THE AUTHOR

Matthew T. Dawson is the Lead Pastor at Journey Church in Huntersville, NC, where he's served for the past 20 years. With 25 years of pastoral ministry experience spanning multiple churches, Matt has dedicated his life to helping believers discover that Christianity isn't just about believing right—it's about living ON purpose FOR purpose.

Matt's ministry is built on what he calls "Truth & Joy"— uncompromising biblical truth delivered with laughter, compassion, and the kind of authenticity that makes faith feel accessible rather than intimidating. He's not interested in watering down Scripture to make people comfortable, but he's also convinced that encountering God's truth should be life-giving rather than life-draining. That combination of theological conviction and relational warmth has shaped everything from his preaching to his writing.

Over two and a half decades of pastoral ministry, Matt has discovered that most believers aren't lacking information—they're lacking activation. They know about spiritual gifts in theory but have no idea how to deploy them in practice. That gap between knowledge and action is what *Gifted: On Purpose For Purpose* is designed to bridge.

Beyond his local church, Matt has trained pastors and church leaders throughout the Carolinas and internationally through his work with The Cypress Project, bringing practical ministry training to leaders in Haiti, the Dominican Republic, and Kenya. His heart for equipping extends globally because he believes every believer—regardless of geography or circumstance—deserves to understand the supernatural capacity God has placed within them.

Through his YouTube channel **"Set Free Stay Free with Matt Dawson,"** he provides accessible biblical teaching and practical ministry resources that help believers move from lazy faith to living hope. Whether unpacking spiritual gifts, addressing theological questions, or providing pastor training content, Matt's approach remains consistent: make truth clear, make it practical, and make it possible for everyday people to walk in extraordinary purpose.

Matt lives with his family in North Carolina, where he continues to challenge believers to stop preserving their spiritual gifts like collectibles and start using them like the powerful tools God designed them to be. When he's not writing, preaching, or training leaders, you'll find him cheering loudly for people discovering that the supernatural life they've been longing for has been inside them all along.

Connect with Matt:

- Website: MattDawson.tv
- YouTube: Set Free Stay Free with Matt Dawson: YouTube.com/@mattdawsontv
- Journey Church: TheJourneyOnline.com
- The Cypress Project: CypressProject.org

DISCOVER, DEVELOP, AND DEPLOY YOUR SPIRITUAL GIFTS.

Join Matt Dawson for a transformative journey from spiritual gift discovery to Kingdom impact.

- Identify your unique spiritual gift mix through comprehensive assessment and biblical teaching

- Break through the myths and misconceptions keeping you from your God-given purpose

- Learn to recognize where your gifts meet the world's deepest needs

- Develop a personal action plan for living ON purpose FOR purpose

Stop Wondering About Your Purpose. Start Walking In It. Join The GIFTED Masterclass[IP]

MattDawson.tv/GiftedMasterclass

HELP YOUR AUDIENCE DISCOVER THEY'RE GIFTED ON PURPOSE FOR PURPOSE.

Churches and organizations worldwide are eager to hear from Matt Dawson as he helps believers understand their divine design and step into their God-given calling.

Matt will captivate, challenge, and catalyze your audience to stop settling for ordinary faith and start living the GIFTED life God designed them for.

BOOK MATT FOR YOUR NEXT CONFERENCE, RETREAT, OR CHURCH EVENT.

MattDawson.tv/Speaking

www.ingramcontent.com/pod-product-compliance
Lightning Source LLC
LaVergne TN
LVHW011810060526
838200LV00053B/3724